Creating & Changing Mindsets

Movies of the Mind

STRATEGIES FOR LONG-TERM IMPACT

Upon Change and the Acts of Achievement,
Motivation, and Relationship Building

By
Dr. Robert K. Greenleaf

Greenleaf & Papanek **Publications**

Creating & Changing Mindsets
Movies of the Mind

STRATEGIES FOR LONG-TERM IMPACT
Upon Change and the Acts of Achievement,
Motivation, and Relationship Building

Printed in the United States of America.

Greenleaf & Papanek **Publications**

Contact Information

Dr. Robert K. Greenleaf
P.O. Box 186
Newfield, Maine 04056
207.793.8675 tel
207.604.0089 cell

bob@greenleaflearning.com
www.greenleaflearning.com

Doris Wells-Papanek
1521 Heritage Court
Lake Forest, Illinois 60045
847.615.9957 tel
847.615.9958 fax

doris@tailoredlearningtools.com
www.tailoredlearningtools.com

ISBN: 0-9767860-2-8

Acknowledgments

A distinguished colleague on the west coast.

Dr. Gary Phillips
National School Improvement Project
P.O. Box 1234
Issaquah, WA 98027

Creating & Changing Mindsets
Movies of the Mind

Table of Contents

SECTION ONE	**INTRODUCTION**	page 1
	The Basis	page 2
	The Mindset	page 3
	The Magic of Movies	page 4
	Impacting Movies Creates Change	page 5
	The Vehicle ~ Emotion	page 6
	The Connection ~ Movies and Actions	page 7
SECTION TWO	**THE FOUR FOUNDATION MINDSETS**	page 8
Foundation Mindset #1	**I Am Capable**	page 9
Foundation Mindset #2	**Today Connects With Tomorrow**	page 11
Foundation Mindset #3	**I Make a Difference**	page 13
Foundation Mindset #4	**Someone Believes In Me**	page 14
	A Story ~ From Zero to Four	page 16
SECTION THREE	**INTRODUCTION TO SEVEN STRATEGIES**	page 20
Strategy 7	**The Power of Rituals**	page 22
	Applications	page 29
Strategy 1	**Cognitive Dissonance**	page 33
	Applications	page 41
Strategy 2	**Create-A-Vision**	page 45
	Applications	page 53
Strategy 3	**Challenging Activities**	page 58
	Applications	page 65
Strategy 4	**"As-If"**	page 69
	Applications	page 76
Strategy 5	**Paradoxical Intentions**	page 81
	Applications	page 87
Strategy 6	**The Virtue of Vulnerability**	page 90
	Applications	page 97

SECTION FOUR	**ACTIVITIES FOR WORKING WITH YOUNG PEOPLE**	page 100
Activity 1	**Celebrate Improvement**	page 102
Activity 2	**Don't Be Afraid to Fail**	page 108
Activity 3	**Developing Identity, Self Worth. Who Am I?**	page 114
Activity 4	**Breaking Patterns ~ Changing the Status Quo**	page 120
Activity 5	**I Don't Matter**	page 126
Activity 6	**Inviting Mistakes ~ Fear of Failure**	page 132
Activity 7	**Make Me Feel Worthwhile**	page 138
Activity 8	**Appreciation**	page 144
	Bibliography	page 151
	About the Author	page 155
	Book Order Form	page 156

SECTION ONE

Introduction

If people acted out of simple logic this book would not have been conceived if rational behavior was the basis for human interaction, the mysteries of learning and development might not loom in such large wonderment. Yet, there are some strategies to assist. The questions have long been "for how long will this practice be in place?" or "will this change last?"

Most of us do not come from, nor live, storybook lives. Just the same, we've conjured up some idyllic notions of what life "*is supposed*" to be like. It is our distance from actualizing such mental pictures which causes disappointment, if not stress in our lives. This book speaks to the issues of how the mind works to accept input, read its environment and how it deals with feelings. Truly, the brain is a complex system of input, storage, and retrieval. It is largely our greatest frontier of exploration. Once we come to understand the immense powers of the human mind, keys to many other mysteries may be unlocked.

First things, first. After all, Monday morning is just around the corner and you've got to get back to the workplace. The familiar people, situations, and issues will be waiting. This book is the beginning of a journey which will serve to address how to make your tomorrows a little bit better than your yesterdays. If we employ strategies which impact people's actions in a sustained manner, then tomorrow may become a bit easier… and more pleasant for all of us!

Some of the strategies put forth in this book will fit your style and circumstance like a glove. Super! Some will feel awkward ~ especially at first. Some will feel uncomfortable. That's O.K. Leave those alone for the time being. Go back to them when you sense you are ready or feel more inclined. At times, some may feel corny or silly ~ a bit juvenile. These have the greatest potential, if you stick with them. People will balk and resist… but down under the façade of acculturated, social reactions… they love it!

And so will you! **Hang in there!**

The Basis

The REAL Logic

Analogics. That's right. Not logic, but *ana*logic. It's another form of logic ~ the one out of which most of us interact. Its basis is in how the brain functions to interpret, store, retrieve, and relate the milieu of daily stimuli that comes our way. We can attend, but to a small fraction of it all. Thus, our brain is equipped to sort out much (below the level of full consciousness) and relegate a great deal to autonomic and automatic types of interpretations. We call them patterns or routines. The kind of regular, repeated occurrences that happen so consistently, with strikingly similar responses, that we are hardly aware such is taking place. This is a vital, important aspect of human development. If we were not equipped to do this, we would be so consumed with daily living and the most base of survival inputs that we would have far too little time to plan, prepare, and imagine the possibilities future times may hold. This is where the brain and mind intersect. The world of psychology, our instincts (genetic and learned), and our environment meld into expectancies and experiences that guide most of our upcoming lives.

The Mindset

Holding On

It is exciting, yet frustrating at times. When change finally becomes necessary, many still hold fast to former, suitable reactions, and behaviors. That's where Mindsets come in. We all have them… the hundreds of experiences and understandings about a given area or topic or interest. We've practiced *trial and error* in the past and settled on a "best" way of doing things. That's being efficient… until it becomes time to look at alternatives. Then we tend to hold on to the effective strategies ~ even after we understand they have outlived their usefulness. We truly are "creatures of habit!"

The Magic of Movies

Making Movies

Each mindset we hold has been constructed through multiple, related "Movies." Every mind runs two types of movies (mental pictures).

One is of ***past*** life experiences. These are the ones which provide a rich history of things we've tried, and all that has gone into establishing the policy or practice as we know it today. If I were to ask you what you did on the last Fourth of July holiday, you could recall some events, travel, people... perhaps the weather. You created a movie of some things about the day, which were stored in a "loop" of familiar, categorically similar issues (holidays, days-off from work, family outings, travel, etc). In recalling the 4th of July (the most recent past), other similar or related occurrences are likely to come to mind easily as well ~ if not automatically! These are the times we project into the unknown, uncertain, or untried arenas. Keeping with the example above, I might ask you what you will be doing on the next 4th of July. Your mind would run through both past ideas as well as potential shifts, changes and new possibilities in responding. So, with ease, our minds run mental pictures... movies which we draw upon. Whether stored movies of the past or imagined happenings, we explore options from the tried and true to the outlandish. Then we make decisions.

Impacting Movies Creates Change

Communicating for Impact

The mind is not easily influenced by verbal means. We've all heard it before. We've been through so many new supervisors that we no longer believe the situation is really going to change much ~ so why invest?

We all resist some things. *Actually, most people resist change ~ because they'd be fools not to!* No one wants to be unnecessarily burdened with extra work or new practices if they are not going to prove beneficial or to last. *And,* most don't. So, if you're playing the odds ~ it's a safer bet that nothing will come of it, than the notion that this time it's really going to make a difference. Let's explore how it works ~ so we can determine how to address items of interest or need.

Recent research that indicates only 7% of our influence comes from the words we use in communicating to others. Another 38% of our impact is from voice tone, inflection, and facial expression. A whopping 55% originates from our posture. How we carry our frame has a greater impact upon the message we send to others than any other combination of things we may do. Think of it. If this weren't true, then no one would ever have to look at another person while requesting something or instructing them. If words and inflection alone consistently produced the impact we wanted, we would not have to repeat our selves so often ~ if at all!

The reality of it all is that something as simple as adjusting your chin (up or down by one-quarter inch) conveys a very different "message" to the receiver. Our posture paints the big picture ~ the major component of what is emoted. It is the vehicle for communication. What we "**emote**" in our communication "carries" the intended message.

The Vehicle

Emotion is the Vehicle

The meaning of emotion here is not the simple happy or sad stuff. Those are real, however not what the focus is here. The power of a message is carried through what is emoted, not what is said. If your posture is slumping, shoulders droopy, it is difficult to believe the statement, "I'm glad to be here." Likewise we would have trouble with, "I'm depressed" while in a victory stance with both fists clenched high above your head. The components of the message (tone, expression, words, and posture) must be consonant ~ or the receiver will pick up on the dissonance and the posture will have the most impact.

Emotion (or what is emoted) is dependent upon the recipient as well. The impact of our message will be directly related to the amount of personal meaning (interest, connection) contained, as perceived by the receiver. It matters far less what you and I believe to be true or important than what the target person believes. If we can both explain the idea or desired action well *AND* connect the message with something of personal interest to the recipient, the chances of truly impacting their thinking and actions will dramatically increase. Thus, logic is seldom the key ~ making connections is. Often, it is the strategies which are not the typically rational ones that impact and motivate.

The Connection

The Movies and the Actions are Connected

The reason it is so important to alter an old movie or create a new movie is that the movies that run in the mind are directly connected to the external expressions of the individual. These are the behaviors and attitudes that we observe. So often we address issues and concerns through the behavior of the person. While this is not wrong, it is incomplete. Any result is most often short lived. If the behavior is altered and the internal movie remains unchanged, then we have likely achieved temporary compliance, not change. It is only a matter of time before the old, less desired behavior returns.

Since actions and movies are connected, it is important to develop strategies that impact both. This way, sustained change is more likely to happen. We are all too familiar with the numerous efforts of rewards, incentives and disciplinary actions which influence (usually suppress) behaviors for relatively short periods of time. Revamping an existing procedure every month or two to try and maintain effectiveness is a burden and energy drain on the supervisor, parent, or educator that needs to be avoided. If we keep the internal movie in mind when we observe the actions and dispositions, then we might approach issues differently. If our manner serves to assist someone with lasting efforts toward more productive behaviors, then everybody wins.

SECTION TWO

The Four Foundation Mindsets

The Basis of Motivation, Esteem, & Achievement

The following pages outline the "Four Foundation Mindsets" in prose and graphics. Each is a cornerstone for individual or group achievement, motivation and esteem. These represent the essential components of a healthy attitude, and a "can-do" disposition. When we hold all four, we are nearly invincible ~ believing we can do just about anything. We are constructively seeking options, welcoming change for its benefits and working to make things better. However, when we are lacking and have few or none, we need little outside influence or pressure to fall flat on our face. We become more negative and pessimistic about possibilities and intentions. We expend time and energy in resisting and avoiding the new and different, in part out of fear that we will fall short of desired goals or even fail completely.

The condition of the mindsets within an individual is situational. We all have times when all four are present and other arenas where few, if any, remain. It is when an employee has few in the workplace that productivity becomes an issue. Similarly, groups can foster overall feelings associated with the mindsets. Committees or project teams often develop an overall sense of "can-do"... or discouragement. The foundation mindsets are equally important to groups as they are to individuals.

The job of the manager, team leader or even co-worker is to help install the foundational beliefs that encourage and enable both individuals and teams to move forward. If we believe in the following fundamental concepts, then motivation is abundant and results are only moments away. Building the Four Foundations Mindsets in an employee (a child, a significant other) will pay tremendous dividends down the line.

1. We are capable
2. Efforts today connect with outcomes tomorrow
3. I/We, specifically, make a difference
4. Someone (in a position to matter) believes in us.

As you read through these pages, reflect upon times when you had each of the foundation mindsets intact... and times or situations in which few or none were present. Take a moment to notice the feelings that accompany the presence or absence of each. This may serve to help understand others and their actions ~ from a different viewpoint.

Creati

Foundation Mindset #1

I Am Capable

How I *see* myself determines how I *act*.

If I *feel* capable, I then *act* capable.

If I *feel* unworthy, I *act* in ways that will make me unwanted.

If I *feel* interested, I *act* in ways to express my interest.

If I *don't care*, I *act* without care and consideration.

If I *feel* like a winner, I *act* like a winner.

It is no secret that people who feel good about themselves and their abilities approach situations in constructive manners. Likewise, people who feel unable or unworthy are less likely to take charge, to risk and to venture without being driven and monitored. Thus, the basis for this Foundation Mindset:

"If I FEEL ____________, I ACT ____________."

(important)   (important)

Each of us can think of a situation in which we feel capable. Be it work, home, social, or recreational, we all can do something well. When immersed in this type of activity, we feel able ~ confident. This basis enables us to try more things at which we might otherwise be timid. We tend to venture, to risk... and most likely succeed. If we fall short, it is not a major ordeal. We have a rich history of ability in this arena, thus we persist and ultimately prosper.

We also have circumstances in which we do not feel capable. For most, this puts us at-risk of not believing in our potential success. Instead we become doubters, cautioning every step forward. We crawl to an uncertain success or timidly delay, fearing failure. In some cases we do succeed, yet do not credit our ability ~ as we do not believe we were responsible for the achievement. Other times we fail outright and confirm our suspicions... that we really are inept. AND, the cycle of a missing or negative mindset continues.

Helping a co-worker, subordinate or even family member to build their repertoire of can-do "movies" is vital to long-term feelings of personal capability and success. If we employ strategies to help those about us become more productive as employees (and individuals in their personal lives as well) we stand a far greater chance of seeing sustained changes in behavior. Substantially, these changes represent long range differences in performance and disposition that have payoffs for the employee, their supervisor and company productivity. Everybody wins.

Recognizing this Foundational Mindset as "intact" or "deficient" can be the first step toward helping someone move closer to achieving their capabilities. Embracing the "I can" mindset leads us to success far more readily than "I'm not sure." As Charles F. Kettering stated,

"If you think you can, you're right. If you think you can't, you're right!"

Foundation Mindset #2

Today Connects With Tomorrow

The efforts I am investing today are connected to the outcomes I hope to have happen in my tomorrows.

I must believe that given reasonable effort... a desired outcome can happen.

- Do I have a vision of what I would like to become... or have happen in my life?
- Do I believe my actions today are contributing toward reaching this vision ~ or at least a portion of the goal?

If so, I have greater motivation to invest.

It may be at a level that is not always foremost on our minds, but we all do it. We all search for meaning. Whether in our daily lives, our work or our discretionary time, we all seek to capture activities and relationships which create or connect with meaning for us. Simple... not easy.

If we have chosen a career which is rewarding and fulfilling for us, we are considered fortunate. We escape the meaninglessness, the boredom of putting in our time and hanging around until something better comes along ~ maybe retirement. The same is true in our private and social lives. If we understand the relationship between our efforts and probable outcomes, we are far more apt to make a commitment. We weigh our investment of energy against the odds for return dividends. If we see a connection that has a high enough probability, we venture forth. If not, we are unmotivated to participate. The same parallels exist at home, at work, and for children at school.

If I understand how my job fits into the scheme of the organization ~ and believe that it is important, I am more likely to want to do it well. Beyond the mere job description lays a larger factor... ME. Even if I believe my job is important, I will be less likely to apply my abilities if I do not believe my efforts have a definite connection with future outcomes.

Bottom Line

1. If I know and believe in what I am trying to achieve, I am more motivated to do my best.
2. If I understand how my present (daily) efforts connect with possible and even probable desirable outcomes, I am more motivated to do my best.

Mid-life crisis is a time when someone no longer makes connections between daily trials, efforts, and hassles and purposeful, meaningful outcomes for their future. When we lose sight of our goal (our reason for investing the energy and time today), then each obstacle and unforeseen issue becomes a problem to bear. The future orientation turns feelings of enduring a situation into a possibility with some degree of worth. Now any efforts become an investment, rather than a necessary evil ~ or worse ~ a total burden. Students need to believe that today's efforts will contribute toward something meaningful in their tomorrows. There's no guarantee; however, believing there is possibility changes much!

Foundation Mindset #3

I Make A Difference

Where is the "locus of control" in my life?

What I do today counts for something. I matter.

We come and go. We do our thing. Others do theirs. Amidst the tumult and busy times lies a cornerstone to motivation and feelings of worth. It's about **IMPACT.** Does anything I do matter? Did the fact that I was there make a difference to someone or something... somehow?

If we believe a difference is made when we show up... then, we matter. All of us want to count for something. Still we question our worth, often. Do we really count for something? How do I know that what I do makes a worthwhile impression on outcomes around here?

When we help another to see how they really do influence their environment and/or those about them, their motivation to continue, to contribute and to get involved is heightened. We all need a sense of purpose about our efforts. People who are motivated to achieve, to make earnest efforts toward a desired end ~ believe not only that they have the *ability* to make a difference... but, that they *actually do*!

It's a great feeling of confidence and of being a needed member of this group ~ to know you are truly a part of a team that makes a difference. Understanding that I have an active role in making things happen is gratifying, esteem building and motivating.

Yes, I do "cause" outcomes in my life. It doesn't all just "happen" to me ~ I influence the results ~ the reality which becomes my success.

Foundation Mindset #4

Someone Believes In Me

"You may feel like things are not going your way right now. Don't give up. I'm with you, you can make it!" You're O.K.

Research indicates that even a child who does not believe in her/himself *will* succeed... if s/he has two adults in her/his life who do believe in her/him (and express it). There is something magical about another human being demonstrating a complete faith in who we are and what we are capable of accomplishing. "You can do it;" "I believe in you;" "I won't give up on you;" "You matter;" and "Hang in there;" if sincere, send a message of belief. It is a testimony to the power of faith and support from others that we continue at junctures which might have resulted in decisions to give up.

We all have a close friend ~ a personal confidant who believes in us. They accept us for who we are. *AND* they often recognize the potential within us, even when we do not. While we are free to doubt our own capabilities, and usually do so, others are less susceptible to our fears and anxieties.

We all need to believe we matter (Foundation Mindset #3). If this belief comes from inside ourselves, our need to have it reinforced externally may be less impinging. However, few are of such strength and inner peace. Outside affirmations provide a much needed support that bolsters and reassures our views. When people who are in a position to know us, our work and our character indicate that we are capable, we are encouraged to persist beyond where we otherwise would have ventured.

Many times, under the surface facades, we know we can do something. What we don't know is if *others* believe we can do it. An expression from another "who would know" or whom we hold credible, can serve to build the confidence we need to attain optimal performance... sometimes to even begin.

Ultimately, we are better adjusted if our strength comes from a personal conviction and sense of worth. While we're waiting for a colleague or student to create this within him/herself, we might offer some support. We find what we look for. If we look for the areas of potential and promote these avenues, we are far more apt to find improvement and success than if we look for and find the otherwise obvious deficiencies. While we don't always "*feel like doing this for another*," each of us would thoroughly appreciate someone making the effort on our behalf.

Who can you be a "**potential mirror**" for... reflecting back the traits and abilities which would help them to realize untapped personal resources?

The dividends are immense.

A Story

From Zero To Four ~ Foundation Mindsets

The following is a story. It depicts a time when the author was lacking all four foundation mindsets, what he did and what the result was. Though it does not capture something directly from a business setting, it does have strong parallels to what can happen. This review covers a circumstance where someone went from having none… to having all four mindsets in place. While many cases will not occur either this rapidly or with this completeness, the illustration is graphic as to potential. Oh, one other thing. This story is a true one.

There I was, sitting at my desk. I had risen to be an assistant superintendent of schools in just a brief seven years in the business… the picture of success for so many. Yet like most, I was not good at everything. We all have strengths and shortcomings.

No big deal. The question was, "Are the areas of underdevelopment in my life the ones that do or don't matter to me?"

It was no "great shakes," but I had always wanted to be able to develop my artistic side ~ yet had failed miserably as a youth to show any promise. It's not that learning to draw well was critical ~ or even important to my work. I simply wanted to be able to draw without embarrassment or feeling like my expressions were the equivalent of a four year old's. We all have things we want to do but are not good at. Most of us learned long ago that we couldn't do some things well: sing, draw, dance, work in isolation, work with large groups of people, work in tightly supervised arenas or work in situations with nebulous parameters. Whatever it was, we learned it as a matter of fact and have believed it ever since.

Well, that was before this crazy flyer arrived. The mail positioned a "You Can Learn to Draw Portraits Like an Artist" brochure on my desk. It claimed that I didn't need ability or past experience. It touted Dr. Betty Edwards, author of the book, Drawing on the Right Side of the Brain, as the instructor. Now, I didn't believe I could accomplish such gains, but I had conducted numerous workshops on right/left brain processing and knew there could be something to the approach. Resist as I tried, I had to call. California. That's right. That's where the workshop was to be held. A guy named Hal answered the phone.

"Hello, this is Hal at the Brain Ed. Center, Long Beach."

I said, "Hal, this is Bob ~ from Maine. I read your brochure..." and began to snicker under my breath ~ at the thought that I had actually called.

He inserted, "You can do it. You can learn to draw portraits you would display on the wall ~ in five days. Come on out."

Emphatically I replied, "I can't draw at all."

The response was a simple, "Good, this is for you, come on out."

I said, "Hal. On a good day I can make stick figures look like they're moving."

"Come on out. We'll teach you to do portraits in five days," was all he said.

Ever had the feeling? I had to go. Can you imagine telling your spouse that you are going to spend a healthy sum of family savings to fly to California, pay tuition, room and board, stay a week and learn how to draw?

So here I was on the plane, with the absence of any of the four foundation mindsets: 1. I did not believe I was capable; 2. I did not really believe the week's investment would make the transformation happen; 3. I was sure I could not make the difference necessary to bring it about; 4. No one cared. They all thought it was absurd to even *want* to go ~ never mind actually doing it. I was, what is commonly called, *At-Risk*. Somehow I persisted and showed up Monday morning on location.

Dr. Edwards entered the room with a hired model trailing closely behind her. After a polite "Good morning," she drew attention to the model (now seated in front of the room) and told us we had forty-five minutes to draw her. I instantly objected, saying that she had forgotten to teach us how, that she was supposed to do that first! Dr. Edwards was not amused. Forty-five minutes later I had drawn a most pathetic, fourth grade facsimile of the model.

The next instruction was to put our paper before us on the table and then look directly to one side at our hand and draw it ~ complete with every hair, line and detail. Needless to say, mine came out looking like a mess. When I saw her coming toward my station I quickly inserted some finger-like protrusions from the balled up darkness at the center of my paper and returned to the directed posture.

She came by and said, "That's terrible."

I said, "I know. That's why I'm here!"

She objected, "No. It looks like a hand. You can't do this activity and actually draw your hand."

I was obviously perplexed. She explained, "Your drawing of the model looked about the same as the drawings you did back in elementary school. Everyone's drawings do. You see, most of us really tried hard to learn to draw well, but it never happened. We filled the refrigerator with repeated attempts that never improved. Given these failures and a few comments from others about our poor performance, we finally believed we had no ability. We simply could not draw because we had no genes to enable the skill. What really happened is that you got to a certain point and no longer progressed, so you believed you couldn't go further. Today, you sit here with a movie playing in your head that says 'I can't draw."

Suddenly I understood. We were going to work on developing a set of new movies that would gradually go from "I can't" in mode to "Maybe, some easy things" to "Yes, I can draw!" I buckled down for the duration. We drew the most tedious of things; our foot, a spoon, our thumb, a brick, etc. Each one removing the old movie further from its resting place, supplanting a new one ~ which began to believe in the progress.

Each day we learned one skill. That's it. If you can hold a pencil, you can learn the skill. On the third day we learned the skill of "negative space." Dr. Edwards entered the room with a bushy plant.

"Do you see the plant?" she asked. We nodded. Then she continued, "Don't draw it. Instead, draw the spaces in between the leaves and stems of the plant." [This is called negative space].

So, we began drawing the shapes and proximities of the spaces where you could see *through* the plant. Sure enough, 90 minutes later, we all had drawn what now became the image of the plant, but like a photographic negative. Neat! My movies soared with the success. Now I believed I could draw. Not portraits, but *things*… quite well. At the end of the fourth day another model was brought into the room and placed before us. I was terrified. Plants ~ O.K., but not people ~ not yet!

"You have two hours. Draw her," said Dr. Edwards. And we did. By the end of the day we each had a drawing of the model which looked pretty good. I was elated! Even the art teacher I had met on day #1 came by and told me how well she thought I'd done. Movies were being created and altered at a furious pace and I was beginning to believe I really could draw.

On the final day we learned the skill of *light and shadow*. Then, we were taken into this large room with no windows, and the lights were turned off. The model sat before us with a hat on his head and one light shining against half of his face. We had two hours. And what glorious drawings did we construct! All 60 of us! Everyone drew him well. Attending to our learned and developing skills was all it took. We had each overcome a movie we had been living for many years. In five short days, the "No-Way" movies of 25 years had been replaced with "Can-do" images. I now had all four foundation mindsets in place:

#1 I truly believed I was capable at drawing

#2 I had invested in today and was reaping benefits the tomorrows bring

#3 I believed I had made a difference in both my life and others during the week ~ and that I could continue to help others as a result

#4 People cared about my progress and ultimately, my success. I had gone from having none to having all four of the foundation mindsets.

My outlook, based on the new movies I had created, was "can-do" rather than "can't do." My behaviors and attitude toward potentials and possibilities in art and drawing had shifted dramatically.

Now, finally, I was a contributing, positive factor for others around me when it came to art ~ and it spread from there. If I can overcome the long tried belief about lacking capabilities in drawing... what could be my next challenge? I had learned something far greater than drawing. I had learned that I do not have to accept "can't" in my life. I can change my position, my perception, and my outward capabilities.

If interested in the program on drawing, write to:

Center for the Educational Application of Brain Hemisphere Research
California State University at Long Beach
1250 Bellflower Blvd., Long Beach, CA. 90840-3501

SECTION THREE

Introduction to the Seven Strategies

This section of the book identifies seven strategies that can be used to impact the movies of the mind, and thus, attitudes and behaviors. The information related to each strategy will encompass several pages. The first page will be analogical ~ the intent being to capture a feeling ~ the essence of the idea to be outlined. After this a concise, dictionary-type definition of the strategy will be provided.

Next, the "**Purpose**" component briefly states the function of the overall concept. It is followed by the "**How**" component. Here, the concept is further developed to build more understand of why it can be effective and how to use it to impact a situation. These paragraphs provide the context for better making use of the actual strategies and applications provided.

The "**In Practice**" section provides some applications from experience in workplace settings. Following this will be an "**Off The Wall**" section. Its purpose is to supply another perspective ~ something on the lighter side of life!

"**Highlights**" is a brief synopsis or reminder of an important element. Next, "**From The Sideline,**" is intended to offer another perspective on the subject from a variety of sources. Concluding commentary about the strategy, "**Weighing the Facts: What Greenleaf Learning Says**" is a bottom line with respect to what this is all about.

After the above elements, "**Implementing the Process**" provides an explanation of the activity that follows. This format provides a leader, facilitator, or teacher with additional background information toward conducting activities with their class, a department, school faculty, or the entire organization. Thus, each set of elements offers a comprehensive view of the strategy or concept under consideration. The variety of ideas and approaches included are intended to be useful as one implements this process.

Finally, "**Applications**" offer several ideas within a range of approaches and perspectives that are intended to help you glean ways of generating activities that are tailored to your situation and needs. Review all the items offered, then make adjustments or combine elements of one or more to form an activity that will be effective in your setting, for your purposes.

Strategy 7

An Important Note

You will undoubtedly note that Strategy Seven is placed first in the series of strategies. While this is a bit unusual, it is deliberate. Each of the strategies is designed to impact mindsets through engaging one or more movies of the mind. While other approaches have been very successful, my experiences with the strategy of RITUALS have produced the most remarkable, lasting results. Thus, my partiality is showing!

All seven strategies serve to engage the movies that cause one to take a closer, perhaps different look at what had previously been dismissed or decided. However, it is the practice of Rituals that has tended to cement the changes I have undertaken. It will do us little good to expend energy to foster change and improvement if everything resorts back to "the way it was" prior to beginning. We need to implement strategies that help to sustain the desired differences. This is why rituals are so important. I have often combined several of the other strategies with a component of ritualization. This is why I have placed rituals first.

Read through all seven strategies and note times when you have already used such an approach. Imagine the possible applications of each at some future time. Then… go back and think of each in terms of rituals. What consistent, regular, without-fail ritual could you attach to the efforts, which would serve to strengthen the new practice, behavior, or idea?

Strategy 7

The Power of Rituals

Ritual Defined: 1. A regular, consistent, same time-same station practice or activity that sends a clear message ~ "THIS is important around here." 2. An activity that happens, no matter what. 3. Something which is valued by virtue of routine inclusion. Nothing gets in the way of doing this!

Purpose

To imbed new, more productive behaviors which are valued and desired.

How

Conduct a simple act for *twenty-one times in a row* ~ without interruption in occurrence. If it is a daily act, then I must occur twenty-one days in a row. If weekly, then twenty-one weeks, etc. It is best to attaché the act to a fixed time, place, day of the week, event, etc. (i.e. every Tuesday at 1:30pm, every day at dinnertime, every time students come in from recess, etc.).

The shorter, easier the task, the better the chance of success. The act must support or exemplify the desired value. Deep it simple. Keep a record of completion, occurrence (daily or weekly, etc.). Be deliberate. Be consistent ~ and be successful!

Most rituals are "same time, same station, save everything." One variation is called a "floating" ritual. These are *If-Then* situations. If someone does "X," then "Y" immediately occurs. They may not be tied to the clock (a certain time of day) or an expected event (recess, lunch, to begin a meeting). These could happen many times in a single day ~ or only once in a week or two. In any event, IF the precipitating *action* occurs, THEN the immediate "*reaction*" must take place… without fail. Some examples follow.

In Practice

A principal at an elementary school implemented the following rituals:

1. "Every morning, I say to myself: 'I work with the best 38 educators in the State of Maine!' I have also, when appropriate, communicated this to colleagues and students and parents."
2. I have made an effort to greet each person who enters the school with enthusiasm, good posture, and a smile, even at the end of a long, tiring day. Results to date: Faculty, staff, and community are spending more time "looking" for what's best, rather than for other things.

Off the Wall

Highlights

Rituals are different from common practice, as they occur without fail.

"Rituals are activities that are repeated... that create a desired emotion or mindset... and communicate, 'That's Important Here!' All [workplaces] have rituals. Some are conducive to [productivity] and some interfere. How the [employer] deals with [absenteeism], discipline, questions, humor, etc., are examples of rituals. Changing the rituals always changes the culture [of the workplace]."

Dr. Gary L. Phillips

Weighing the Facts

What Greenleaf Learning Says...

We often verbalize our intentions to support an idea or practice. We plan and make efforts to identify outcomes which we believe in and that we feel are important. Then comes the tough part. How do we sustain it? How can we keep the enthusiasm or the active involvement going? How do we set up the practice so we don't have to monitor and constantly push it in order to make it happen? What are the chances the new ways will continue?

Rituals send a very strong message that "this is important around here." They represent something that is practiced regularly, without fail... has been given high status. The things we do over and over, that we will not allow other things to interfere with, are the very expression of what we value. Creating a ritual, or connecting a new behavior to an existing ritual, is a way of establishing automatic behaviors that do not require the predisposition... or burden of needing to be policed.

The research tends to support a 21 interval (day/week) repetition prior to the new practice taking complete hold. In our experience, the activity is frequently adopted much before the twenty-one days are over. However, anytime a desired practice falls short of a 21interval repetition, one must begin again, counting from zero, to place the ritual back into action.

Try one. Decide what is valued, honored, or dignified about your workplace. Create a ritual which sends a strong message about its importance. Watch how people not only come to expect it... but rather, support and encourage the ritual.

Implementing the Process

The exercise on the following page is set up to focus upon a situation in your workplace. This is likely to be something that is not happening, which you would like to have happen. Be sure not to write it down in "problem" format. Rather, write down what you *WANT* to see happen (the desired behavior or practice). Though brief in space, include specific factors or details which would help a "fresh pair of eyes" understand the circumstance.

This is most effective when done in a group setting, each member citing his/her situation of choice. Pass the paper to each of three other people for them to respond to the issue outlined at the top of the page. Each reviewer has three lines on which to suggest an activity... *not a solution!*

Solutions are often quick fix ideas that are short lived. Several days or weeks later the remedy loses its momentum and you're back with the same old situation. The response must be in the form of a suggested ritual, a regular, consistent, small action or activity which could be conducted daily or weekly, without fail. Attaching this unobtrusive act to something that already occurs "like clockwork" in the workplace is best; however you can create an independent ritual as well.

Something tied to coffee break, morning arrival, lunch, standard meetings, or other consistent occurrences works well. The intent is to maintain a practice over a period of time, rather than to construct a one-shot deal or set up a complete program to deal with the issue. Remember, you're not interested in short term changes ~ the goal is to alter the situation for a much longer duration.

Identifying Rituals ~ **Activity**

1. Identify a desired outcome that is not taking place regularly right now at your workplace.

2. What consistent, intentional, activity(ies) could take place regularly to support the desired outcome?

Developing Rituals ~ Exercise Template

1. **Issue you'd like to address:**

2. **Possible "ritual(s)" that may be viable:**

3. **Anticipated difficulties or challenges:**

4. **Short term expectations:** There should be none! We aren't looking for instant gratification at the expense of sustained change. We start out expecting this to take a concerted effort and some time, to begin the process of making different choices than in the past.

5. **Long term expectations:**

Applications

For the school, the classroom, the home-school partnership, and for one-on-one relationships.

Recorded uses Weekly, record how science or math is used in daily occurrences and share this with your students or children.

Applied Learning Daily, review a magazine or newspaper and point out how a subject (content area, concept, or objective) is referenced, applied, or related.

Home-School Connections Weekly, orchestrate connections between school and home. On Friday, assign students one or two questions as homework ~ in lieu of the subject areas. Have students ask the question(s) of an adult (parent, relative, business person, community representative). On Monday, discuss or collage the findings. This causes youth and adults to interact ~ one of the most important criteria for school success. It also provides data for studying a topic, community, area of interest, etc. Elementary children might be interested in comparing bedtimes with parents (when did their parents have to go to bed when they were their age?). Middle school youngsters might prefer questions surrounding the boy-girl dating or relationship issues. Secondary students might survey retailers, small businesses, etc. to find out about a topic or theme of study at school (changing world of work ~ "How often have your changed careers? Why ~ why not more or less often?).

A Quote a Day Daily, place a quote in the same location in the classroom. After calling attention to it for several days (even discussing it if you like) students will begin to seek it out, comment on it, and come to expect it to be there. They may even begin to bring in a few quotes of their own!

"Good" Stuff Daily, ask a colleague, spouse, student ~ "What 'good' happened with you today?" The questions will become a daily exercise to be looked forward to. "You find what you look for." If you look for the good... you'll find it!

Two Compliments Floating Ritual 2:1 interactions. The national average of criticisms to compliments is suggested to be about 12:1. Turn the ratio around and create two compliments for each criticism rendered. Tell the class (or your kids at home) that from now on it's alright to be negative, to put someone down, etc., but that each negative statement must be accompanied by an automatic obligation to offer tow specific, sincere comments about the offended person ~ immediately following the negative comment! As soon as a put-down occurs, the person issuing the negative remark must then offer two compliments. No punishment, simply wait. You may even help by suggesting something the person might consider as a positive remark. This way, more people get involved with compliments!

In time, people become less negative an far more constructive when they do offer criticism toward another. If the compliments are specific and sincere, esteem is actually enhanced, even thought a put-down has been levied. Think about it. Most are used to receiving dozens of criticisms for each positive remark. This approach offers an alternative which is shouldered by all, not just you, the adult!

21 Theme Posters Daily, at the beginning of school or to reinforce the onset of a new project, create a simple sign or poster for each of 21 days. In concert with your focus, ask a different question each day ("What have you done to make this the best year yet?" or Has someone helped you today? Have you thanked them?"). Place the new sign on the entranceway (one for each day, as the days come). At the end of the day, place the current one in a conspicuous place in the building. Each day, add the new one to the central location, until all 21 are posted there. By the end of the 21 days, you will hear students remarking about the signs or questions (positive, negative, and predictive of upcoming questions). The goal is to create interest and discussion about the thought presented by the posters, thus any commentary is viewed as having captured their attention. You find what you look for. If the mind is tending to the ideas put forth on the signs ~ then you will tend to observe more behaviors aligned with them than before. What theme or message does your staff wish to emphasize this year?

Poem of the Day Daily or weekly, read a short poem to begin class (or bedtime at home). Ask students to bring in poems they particularly like. Discuss the poem briefly, then move on to the lesson for the day.

Door Greetings Daily, greet your child at the door when arriving home from school. Do not ask "How was school?" You'll get the typical, "Okay." Instead ask, "What went right (well) at school today?" The first response will likely be nondescript, but persist. Insist that the child give you something specific that s/he valued or believed to be important or worthwhile. Keep this up each day, without fail, for three weeks. By the end of this time, your child will arrive at the door expecting you and the question... and will provide the response ~ even before you ask!

Anecdotal Recordings Daily, on a gridded chart with days of the month across the top and desired chores down the left side, record who actually does each of these necessary household tasks. Place the chart in a publicly visible place where all will see it frequently. The ritual becomes the act of daily recording who did each item. The chart becomes a powerful record of notice letting everyone know what the responsibilities are and who has done them. In time, the record will develop the needed assistance more than the continual complaining and nagging ever will!

Articulating Learning End of the week: "What did we do (learn) this week?" Explore what was already known before the week's activities and what new learning took place. Get students in the habit of thinking and reflecting. Identifying what one has learned, accomplished and the gains made are valuable toward acknowledging learning.

Priming Daily, ask students prior to going home, "what was the best part of your day today?" or "What did you learn today?" This is a good review and it arms youngsters with a more specific answer to the questions when they get home... "What did you do at school today?" Students will come to expect the question about 5 minutes before the end of the day ~ and will begin to have responses in mind.

Double Positives Appreciation. Before beginning a regularly scheduled meeting (faculty, administrators, etc.), start the meeting with each person present jotting two positive notes to a colleague (or students, parents, etc.). Index cards can be handed out for this purpose and then sent via interschool mail. If there are 20 people present, forty cards are sent each time a meeting takes place. The ritual is that notes are generated first, then meeting items handles second. The meeting does not begin until all notes are completed.

Reflective Interruptions

Floating ritual. Dealing with interruptions. The door to the classroom is often revolving with many students and people coming and going. It seems we seldom have everyone present for an entire lesson! The ritual develops questioning strategies and makes interruptions a learning experience ~ rather than a break in the flow of the class.

(Knock on the door and person enters) Teacher says, "Excuse me, you have just entered the most important activity of our day ~ learning. Before we take care of your needs, we'd like to ask you a question (meanwhile, the students have been formulating questions to ask of the guest). "Who has a question about what we have been doing today for our guest? (Student asks a question). If answered satisfactorily, the guest is then dealt with and goes about his/her way. If not, then ask a student to take the guest to the learning center (or appropriate place) and help him/her understand the learning of the day, better. When the guest has become involved for a minute or so, then take care of their need.

Try it... you will see students reviewing material in their minds, developing questions, teaching people when necessary and smiling about the interruptions ~ rather than being disrupted without attention to the lesson's objectives.

Meaningful Adult/child Interaction

One of the most powerful influences in a youth's life is the amount of <u>meaningful</u> dialogue s/he has with adults. Schedule your family to eat dinner together at least four nights per week by moving the dinnertime to a time each day when everyone can be present. If a snack is needed at 5pm to help make it to an 8pm dinner time ~ go ahead. If kids must come in from playing at 4:30pm to eat ~ so that all can be together, do it! The importance of being together, talking, and sharing your lives (positives and negatives) will be emphasized.

Home Learning

Weekly, share something you've learned with your child. We say we are all lifelong learners. Talk is cheap, unless you can demonstrate how this is true in your life. Take a moment on a regularly scheduled time to exchange new learning with a youth. First, teacher him/her something new that you have learned and then have him/her teach you something they have learned. Teaching is the most powerful way of learning anything. Engage them in this important act regularly!

Strategy 1

Cognitive Dissonance

Cognitive Dissonance Defined: 1. Disturbing common agreement, thoughts of desired outcomes, or consistency; 2. A variance from common thinking; 3. A combination of ideas or events which cause discord. For example: Often associated with causing one to "double think" something which previously seemed more obvious or automatic.

Purpose

To cause the mind to "fetch up," to rethink... stop long enough to consider the idea, an alternative, a new approach. So often we are on automatic pilot ~ and don't pause sufficiently to really think about the merits of another way. We are busy, hurried, stressed ~ something or other ~ enough to push the work of entertaining an idea aside. The act of creating something dissonant, out of whack, odd, or perplexing enough to cause one to ponder it, is a powerful way to begin the process of considering another "way to be."

Dr. Leslie Hart called it "breaking the proster." It is like breaking the habit, the autopilot, the known convention just long enough to let another idea slide in for a while. The way you know it's happening... is to watch the person's face. Look for a perplexed look, eyes to cross, of the general "huh?" expression. When you see this, you know someone has interrupted the traditional way of thinking long enough to consider its merits or ridiculousness (whichever). Either way, the thought gets a prolonged critique ~ which is exactly what you want!

How

This strategy is not always easy, but it is simple. The goal is to get the eyes to cross (cause the mind perplexity)... to break the proster. Simple statements pointing out the obvious can do this. Also, questions which are sincere, yet directed toward options which were not entertained (even thought to be out of the realm of possibility), can cause the mind to stop and rethink the merits.

The examples which follow will give you an idea of how this works. There are no limits to the ways to do this... it simply takes practice. In the beginning, some forethought and pre-planning of comments to certain students or colleagues will be helpful. In time, they tend to come more easily amidst the daily dialogue.

In Practice

One supervisor realized that all the reminders in the world were not working to help one employee alter his behavior. So he decided to create some dissonance. The next time the employee made the same error, he paid him a sincere compliment on something the employee did not expect. Puzzled, the worker could not help but stand in disbelief, wondering why the usual remark did not come... and furthermore, why a sincere compliment? In a short time, given just a few such remarks, the employee willingly altered his behavior ~ without even one more comment about the initial issue from the supervisor.

Analogical approaches can often dislodge paradigms.

- To chronically complaining employees, "Would you like to begin to improve things today... or wait until next week?"
- To a department with repeated, perennial issues which never seemed to get better, "Please submit a list (or do in a meeting) of ten things each of us could do to contribute to an unhealthy work environment."

Then take the list and publish it, articulate it and share it for consensus. This puts everyone on notice (including management) of what things might be done which are unproductive. If you know this and you still persist, dissonance automatically accompanies the unfavorable act. Sooner or later, the discomfort can serve as a constructive force in altering the behavior.

Off the Wall

"With proper sleep, diet, and care, a healthy body will last a lifetime.

The Clarion

Highlights

"No problem can stand the assault of sustained thinking."

"If we continue to think what we've always thought, we will continue to get what we've always got."

To help a person improve we don't focus on behavior, but we help him/her to:

1. Change his/her mental picture of him/herself
2. Change his/her mental picture of the situation
3. Change his/her mental picture of his/her power to affect/alter the situation

"What I do today is important because I am paying a day of my life for it. What I accomplish must be worthwhile because the price is high."

Weighing the Facts

What Greenleaf Learning Says...

Very little change occurs until something disrupts the equilibrium of a traditional mindset. All the new programs and approaches which can be creatively mustered and implemented will not bring about the sustained changes if a mindset has not been impacted.

Creating cognitive dissonance forces the mind's "movies" open. While this is not necessarily a one-time event, there are several ways to cause "double-think," or a more careful inspection of an idea. Doing the unexpected; varying routines; prompting challenges of growth; and posing questions which come from an unexpected perspective can all foster shifts in what is given credence. People don't want to be unproductive. Rather, they yearn to be valued as a member of some important operation. Often, a little dissonance can shed renewed light upon what is really important for an individual or an entire organization.

Break some routines. Do or say something exactly opposite what is expected and then watch what happens. People maintain a more alert, expectant "edge" when the possibility of something unusual is there. They also think more ~ about ways to make the job more productive and efficient. Prompting people to consider alternatives to convention can bring about healthy exploration of possibilities. It can create a paradigm shift that unlocks doors to new behaviors.

Implementing the Process

The four activities on the next page are intended to explain some approaches to cognitive dissonance as a catalyst to focused thinking and change. One easy way to know that you have impacted a mental "movie" is to observe peoples' eyes as you present a dissonant comment. Their eyes will cross! A funny look will come across their face. Bewildering, perplexing or "I don't believe you said that" type reactions will be seen.

The intent is not to actually bewilder, but the result is profitable. As we implement a scenario which causes someone to consider another point of view... even a perspective 180° from the original stance ~ we encourage deeper reflection of the issues and ask the important question, "Why not?"

When people recall their "best" work or the best job they ever had, we often hear attributes of, "It was never dull (#2-next page)," or "You never knew what would happen next (#1-next page)," or "I learned a lot of new things while I was there (#3-next page)." These are the characteristics which make the workplace exciting and growth oriented.

There are many variations which could be done with each of these four suggestions ~ as well as a host of other approaches to be considered. Give some thought to your routines and expected behaviors... and have a little fun now and then. Often, the most memorable things in our lives come from the unexpected, rather than the planned, thought-out activities.

The Art of Crossing Eyes

Four Approaches to Cognitive Dissonance

1. **Doing the Unexpected**
   Make a list of all the "typical" reactions and routines to everyday happenings and procedures. Then, consider what would occur if you reacted or behaved exactly opposite the usual. If there are one or two options you could use without causing undesired outcomes... why not?!

2. **Variety**
   Once each week, change some aspect of the workplace routine. Have the staff contribute ideas on what each of them would "change for a day" or do differently ~ even on time.

3. **Challenge Activities**
   Are there any activities or tasks which could be delegated to an employee which would cause them to stretch beyond usual demands; to cause growth in a new area; or to get involved with another aspect of the workplace? These prompts point out the disparity between what a person is doing and the potential that lies before him/her.

4. **Analogical Questions**
   Ask questions that reverse the meaning, but spotlight the issue.

   a. "As good a (job title) as you already are, what is keeping you from becoming even better?"

   b. or to a constant complainer, "As bad as things are right now, what's keeping you from becoming cynical?"

   c. or when strategies for progress are scarce, "What could we do that we are not already doing, that would make these circumstances even worse?"

Cognitive Dissonance

"As good a (teacher, parent, friend, etc.) as you already are, what might be keeping you from becoming even better?"

- **With Colleagues?**
- **With Students?**
- **With Clients or Customers?**
- **With Family & Friends?**

Applications

For the school, the classroom, the home, the home-school partnership and for one-on-one relationships, the importance is not in the specific words, but in the delivery. Catching someone in the middle of argument, negativity, stubbornness or unilateral thinking ~ and tossing a little dose of "dissonance" with respect to their line of verbiage, can graphically draw attention to the dominant emotion or style of their delivery.

The strategy works within the person, rather than between the two of you. You simply point out the obvious, then sit back and watch what the mind does with it.

With each of these possible remarks, take a moment to actually play it out in your head. Take time to put yourself in the place of each person and "feel" the impact.

Caution: Be careful not to cross the line to sarcasm. Your tone must be calm and sincere. Remember, your intent here is to foster more productive or alternative ways of thinking. Sarcasm will only cause one to dig in and re-double their efforts to resist change.

To a chronic complainer, in the midst of negative remarks: "As bad as things are around here, what's keeping you from becoming cynical?"

Arlo & Janis Comic Strip

Gene (boy) says to Arlo, "I don't want to go to school." Arlo replies, "But you have to learn." Gene, "Even if I don't want to?" Arlo, "That's what you have to learn!"

To a Student or Adult Persisting with Inappropriate or Foolish Questions

Redirect the student or adult back to the sender. Have them deal with/ or resolve their own conflicts or issues. After a litany of complaints from one student about another, ask, "As difficult as you find 'so-and-so,' what's getting in the way of your friendship?" You see, the litany is not generally rational, so to try and resolve this issue for the student only enlists you as a co-dependent. Such a response places both responsibility on the youth, as well as the suggestion that they are empowered to affect the situation toward a better place... if they choose. It is the last thing they expect to hear from you. They expect you to agree, disagree or give them a solution. Instead you are suggesting they consider dealing with the internal emotion they carry, thus dissonance.

Two Children Bothering Each Other on the Playground

"You must both sit over here until you have each given the other permission to leave and return to play." If two people are disturbed with each other sufficiently to be pestering, pushing, fighting, etc., then while they remain angry, neither will give the other permission to leave. When both have settled down enough to allow the other his/her freedom once again, they are ~ by the very act of reconciliation ~ ready to return to a more productive form of play. They resolve their own issue, without an adult to assess who was right or wrong, etc.

The Feel or Act Relationship

If someone feels stupid, s/he acts stupid. If they feel capable, they act capable. When someone comes to you immersed in their unproductiveness, insufficiencies, etc. ~ they are unlikely to resolve or even seek reasonable solutions. Therefore, we must break the proster ~ the dominant train of thought. "As dumb a thing as you've apparently done, isn't there anything you could do to make your day worse than it already is?" This brings attention to their persistent lament. It also promotes the notion that there are probably worse things that could happen (without saying it).

Youth Begging Parent for a Material Good (T-shirt)

Youth approaches with demonstrative, begging emotion, "Hey, have you seen the new T-shirts. They're so cool! You've got to get me one. Everyone else is getting them. Oh, please ~ you must. I've just got to have one! (on and on). Most often we reply with reason, we balk, we negotiate. This process takes time and is draining. Several times we break down and buy it ~ just to get them off our backs. Other times, we endure the onslaught and are fatigued in spirit and patience at the conclusion. Instead, apply dissonance ~ with equal or similar emotion. Simply reply (you'll have to have a little "actor" in you), "Oh, no! Where have you been? I've been looking all over for you. I wanted to buy you that T-shirt earlier… but I couldn't find you. I'm crushed. I'm beside myself. I don't know what I'm going to do. I spent the money for the T-shirt already and I can't afford it now. Will you please forgive me for my lack of foresight? Please?"

Usually, by the time you have carried on sufficiently to parallel the antics which were delivered to you, the child has backed up a step or two and is looking at you with an oddly perplexed stare of wonderment. Sometimes they simply leave. Others become concerned with your well being and will ask if you are alright. Emotion begets emotion. Be sure they get their full due!

To a Prominent Figure (Leader of an Athletic Club, etc.)

In this example, an avid swimmer; breaking school records; revered by his teammates; supported by many. He wears a skirt and dyes his hair red for the school or team picture. The team has been struggling with attaining a status of worth among the school officials and student body. "As respected as you are, what's keeping you from leading this team to a championship?" Or, "As important as it is for us to bring respectability to the sport of swimming at this school, what do you think you could do to jeopardize everyone's efforts?" This points out that the behavior, though not necessarily wrong, affects more than the individual ~ it has implications for the entire team ~ and the future status of the sport. Right or wrong, each of us must consider both our individual needs as well as those of the group to which we belong.

To a Student Complaining about Receiving a Detention

"If your teacher cared enough about you to give you a detention, then we certainly need to be upset with him/her." This type of response calls attention to both the reaction of the student as well as their option to consider the consequence delivered to them as something other than an act of hostility and unfairness.

The Reverse

Grandpa says to his little 4-year-old granddaughter, who is making a valiant effort to put her shoes on by herself; "Angela, you have your shoes on the wrong feet!" The little girl replies with deliberateness, "No grandpa, these are my feet."

Two Upperclassmen Who were Being Disciplined for the Consumption or Possession or Alcohol on School Grounds

"I would like you both to spend the next three days attending the school's freshmen awareness program on decision making, alcohol, drugs, and choice. Your assignment is to critique each segment of the program for effectiveness, value and potential impact. Please address why the segment will or will not work well. You are not to interact with the freshmen class. Simply attend as 'reporters' and provide the school with your expert views on how to become more effective."

You see, the program obviously had not influenced these two teenagers to any great extent. What better critics than those who were not impacted by the previous efforts! The last thing they suspected (thus dissonance), was to be asked to play an <u>adult</u> role ~ specifically to provide input to the very type of thing they had just violated. In actuality, their input is likely to be more important than that of the participants.

Chronic Complainer

Know someone who has had a charisma bypass... or is gifted in negativity? Each time they put down another person, whether in person or in private discussion about them, immediately offer a positive remark or personal compliment about the complainer.

Emotions are contagious. The predominant emotion of the discussion will prompt others (even if it is just you) to think of happenings which carried similar emotions for you. Often we find ourselves entering the teachers' room feeling upbeat. If the main diet of emotional overtones is negative, your mind will automatically search for events which are consonant with the expressed emotion. Soon, you may find yourself offering quips or stories which parallel the ones you've been hearing.

By persisting to establish a new, more constructive emotion which reverses or alters the emotion of the initial interactions, you can actually cause others to tap into similar experiences. Try it. Enter a room and offer several comments, end on end, which present what's right, what's working, what is great about this place... and watch the reactions. Within a minute they will either join you... or find a less "dissonant" place to go with their complaints.

After Expressing Many Complaints about What is Wrong with this Place

"Would you like to begin to improve things today, tomorrow or next week?" Inherently, the question is pointing out the chronic complaining... along with the choice to do something about it. People are put on notice, without being attacked or engaged in conflict.

To a Department or Group with Perennial Issues

"Please submit a list, by next Friday, of at least ten things each level of this organization could do to contribute to an unhealthy work environment. Next to each one, please state what role your department could reasonably play in helping to bring this suggestion about."

It is important not to do such a thing merely to be reactive. Be serious about the input. Ask for ideas from other departments as well. Publish the list, articulate it frequently, placing it in public places ~ share it with the entire staff. Be in earnest about a desire for everyone to enjoy a pleasant workplace.

Dissonant Thought

"Just because you're paranoid doesn't mean nobody's out to get you."

Ad

"For sale by parents; complete set of encyclopedias. Excellent condition. No longer needed. Adolescent knows everything."

Strategy 2

Create-A-Vision

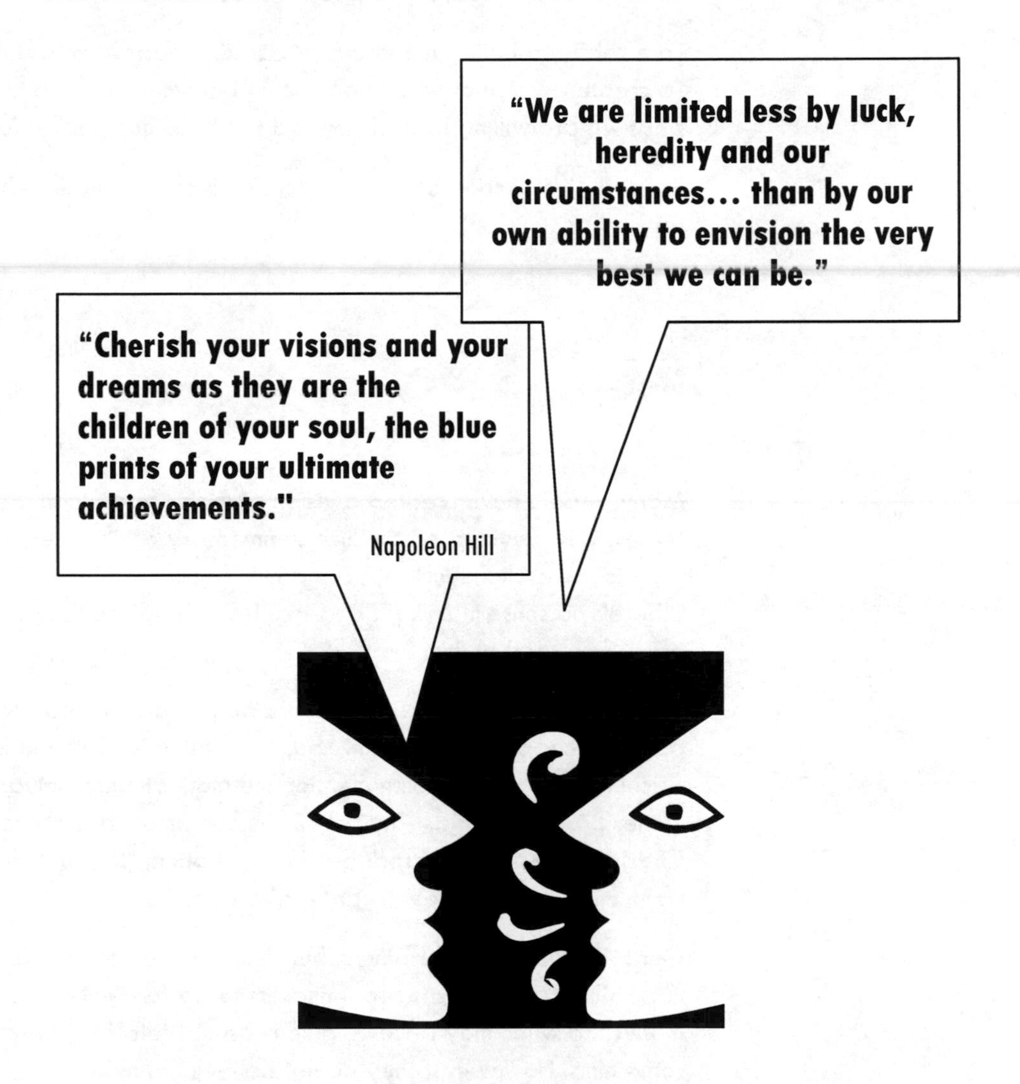

Create-A-Vision Defined: 1. To establish a vision of what we hope to become. 2. To foster ideas about moving toward a life which is "a little bit more" the way you would like it to be. 3. A mindset that projects desired outcomes and activities for the future.

Purpose

Realistic visions foster internal motivation toward a more productive life-style, relationship, workplace, or home. To empower another to take charge of the outcomes in their life, to work toward desired ends with deliberateness.

To establish a belief in oneself, a "can-do" approach to challenges empowers. To create a vision of what we hope to become; what we hope to have happen; what we are willing to work toward provides impetus to action.

Basically, *you find what you look for*. A vision articulates what you're looking for.

How

Many people have created a vision of their life as controlled by external forces. This is evidenced by such commentary as, "I'm never lucky," "Other people have all the luck," "Why doesn't good stuff ever happen to me?" "There's no sense in trying or caring: it won't happen anyway" or "I've never been any good at that."

When our vision is impoverished, our beliefs are limited. When our belief in our personal capabilities is diminished, our motivation to even imagine it is discouraged ~ not to even mention the motivation to actually consider it! As James Broughton said, "The only limits are as always, those of vision." Similarly, Charles Kettering was credited with the notion, "If you think you <u>can't</u> you're right. And, if you think you <u>can</u>, you're right."

Our job is not to do *for others*, but to support others in the assimilation of skills, capabilities, and constructive mindsets to do *for themselves*. People are motivated when they believe, give reasonable effort, they can accomplish something. However, if they do not believe, no matter how hard they try, that it can or will happen ~ they will not even begin to try.

Perhaps the greatest poverty one can have is that of an impoverished vision. As was said, "What the mind can conceive, the person can achieve." Young people need a vision which connects their effort of today, with reasonable outcomes of tomorrow.

Create-A-Vision

The best you can envision for yourself as a ____________________ :

- **Share**
- **Articulate**
- **Yourself or Others**

Plan an exciting or productive future.

In Practice

Smith & Hawken is a mail-order marketing firm of top-quality garden tools. They used a technique called scenario-building, developed by Peter Schwartz (author of The Art of the Long View.)

Scenario-building is the process of writing stories about the future. What they did was to create-a-vision of what the world would be and how and where they would fit in. They developed three separate scenarios reflecting the part they would play in each one. "Smith & Hawken sold $200,000 worth of tools the first year and $1 million a year within three years. Today the company does about $50 million annually."

"Image creates desire. You will what you imagine."

J. G. Gallimore

Off the Wall

Highlights

"Image creates desire. You will what you imagine."

James Broughton

Life is Movement

from darkness to light

from thought to action

from ignorance to wisdom

partnered with time
we move
we dance
we grow

But whether we plod through a day

travel the world or fly to the moon

the movements that count
the ones we remember
are gentle shifts within ourselves:

The letting go of an old resentment

the subtle step from fear to trust

the daring leap from the safe and known
to see if we can fly

The softening breath of forgiveness

the guarded move toward self-acceptance

or the lifting of the inner eye
from a clutched and treasured pain
to unsuspected new horizons

Annelou Perrenoud

Weighing the Facts

What Greenleaf Learning Says...

We find what we look for. So simply put, yet overlooked. We all hope for a bright future. Still, so many view their tomorrows in similar fashion to a lottery... as though outcomes are random, or left to chance. If left to outside factors, we are at the mercy of our environment and those around us. If we invest each day, even with the slightest of effort, we cannot only influence the results that come our way, but we can actually begin to shape and direct much of our life-style.

Choices are always ours. Though it does not always feel like we have input or control (like something is being done *to* us), there is always something we can do. Looking toward tomorrow and beyond to determine what we would like our scenario to be like ~ what we would like to have for a living situation ~ or a workplace circumstance, is part of making it happen. We either influence or orchestrate events, or let events determine what we do ~ and sometimes... who we are.

Establishing a vision for the future helps to set targets. Once in place, we can alter a goal if need be. When we are focusing energies in a direction, we have a purpose. Take a person who is emotionally distraught, floundering, wondering what to do with their life ~ and give him/her a goal, sense of purpose, and a realistic vision of what the future can hold... and the problems begin to take care of themselves.

Yes, we find what we look for. What would you like to *find* in your near future?

Implementing the Process

The exercise on the following page is designed to initiate a vision of what you would like to have happen in your life. After you have selected a circumstance (top) respond to the three questions which follow.

1. "What is the best you can sincerely imagine..." is included to allow you to take a moment and reflect upon what you really can expect from your situation. Don't be pie-in-the-sky, but do give yourself credit and state what you think could reasonably happen.

2. The second question: "As good as you are..." ~ what's in the way? Identifying barriers and blocks to accomplishing a goal is equally important to becoming determined. Often, removing barriers is more productive than overpowering the circumstances.

3. Timeliness: What could *you* do... right away, fairly soon and/or over time to make this vision closer to a reality?

It will not happen all at once. You didn't get where you are all at once... or with little time and input ~ so don't expect rapid results. However, do expect movement *IF* you do something each day to bring you a "little-bit" closer to the way you'd like it to be. Invest. The payoffs won't come tomorrow... but they will arrive in due time. You are worth it!

Create-A-Vision Exercise

Select a Role or Situation (at work, home... as a manager, employee)

What is the best you can sincerely imagine for yourself in this role?

As good as you are... what is keeping you from accomplishing this vision?

What could you do to ensure this vision will NOT happen?

What things could you do to begin to make it happen?

Today?	**This Month?**	**This Year?**

As illustrated... what we do TODAY will impact our tomorrows far more than what we simply contemplate. Take action each day... and the tomorrows will take care of themselves!

Applications

Following are ideas for the school, the classroom, the home, the home-school partnership, and for one-on-one relationships. The process of creating a vision in a mind which is not accustomed to them (other than of despair or disenfranchisement) is not a short term happening. However, success begets success. As one begins to believe that possibilities can become *probabilities*... personal investment can blossom. Stick with it!

Consistent Articulation

It is not enough to say, "I told you the day I married you that I loved you. If anything changes, I'll let you know." We need to be reminded...often!

This is also true of anything which we purport to be of value or importance. Things deemed important must be repeated again and again. Clearly, the focus of influence comes out of articulation, not the idea or thought in and of itself. If you really mean it, you must actively promote it. Otherwise, the mind pays little attention to your integrity.

Articulation in a Group

Perhaps the key to establishing a vision which becomes real, that has a life of its own, is articulation. One building administrator began referring to his staff as, "The 44 Best Teachers in the State of Texas." He articulated this at every turn, every meeting, and every encounter. It became the staple comment to be heard everywhere, repeatedly, over and over. Though the staff did not actually believe the 44 best had been attracted to their school, it still gave rise to the thought, "What would it take for me to become one of the 44 best?" And the motivational context of, "What would it take for us to become one of the 44 best?" And the motivational context of, "What would it take for us to become the home of the 44 best teachers in our state?"

As soon as the mind become curious and inquires as to what might be done, what effort might help, what roadblocks are in the way, etc. then people start moving toward the vision. Perhaps slowly at first, but little by little... "Who wouldn't want to be one of the 44 best?"

Exercise

Have your staff or class list 5 words or phrases that best describe their purpose or mission at this school. Post it publicly. It will serve as a casual reminder of why we're here. Call attention to it regularly. Use it or reference it as often as possible. The value comes through repetition and articulation.

Exercise

On page 52 of this book is an exercise for yourself, your class, your child, etc. to "Create-A-Vision." Taking the time to actually imagine what the best can be for you (or a situation) helps to clarify the goal. Our nature is to resist this activity in favor of doing more tangible things. Understanding what we are shooting for improves our odds of hitting the target. If you don't know what you're aiming at, it's far too easy to miss it! Also, knowing what is in your path, what the challenges are, and what things over which you have little or no control is important to planning for eventual success. Let others know what your vision is as well as what the difficulties might be. The act of becoming public is powerful in obtaining internal motivation and external support.

Vision & Expectation

When we hold a believable vision, we come to expect it to happen. A fourth grade teacher finally got the "class from hell." She had heard about them for several years prior to their arrival. Common expectations were to brace oneself and hope for the year to go by rapidly. One day, she went to their files, to investigate the results of former aptitude test, and read in their records the numbers 145, 136, 131, 128, 138, 142, etc. In fact, she discovered her class all fell between the numbers 128 and 145. With this insight she returned to the class and told them she now knew they were extremely capable students, that the foolishness was hereby to come to an immediate halt, that homework was to be completed and passed in the morning without fail, and that the pace of the material to be covered was to increase starting the very next day.

She maintained this for a period of three weeks before the principal came to see her. Astonished, she asked how on earth the teacher had turned the group around. The teacher stated she had become aware that this group was extremely bright, all with I.Q.s between 128 and 145 and that she was going to expect them to live up to their capabilities. The principal asked where the teacher had acquired the information about the student I.Q.s. In showing her the records, the principal noted that the numbers the teacher had referenced were locker numbers, not I.Q.s. Just the same, the vision of seeing the class as bright caused her to treat them as such and to expect much from them, with remarkable results.

Retirement Row

How about having every teacher, in their last three years of teaching, create a vision of the best three years they could realistically imagine... and having the administration and faculty assist the teacher in achieving these things? The final years of anyone's profession ought to be the best, so why not plan for it?

20 Things List

At a designated time, have each person add something to a list of "Things I Want to Do Before I Leave this Earth." We did this at dinnertime. Each night, when all four of us were present, we each would add one entry to our list of "Things to Do..." Mark, age 12, put down such things as parachuting, hang gliding, bungee chord jumping, etc. David, age 9, had several entries of swimming event times ~ the times he was going to achieve in the 1996 Summer Olympics in Atlanta. Mom and Dad also had their list of things they wished to do. The lists were posted where everyone could see them on a daily basis.

Within one year's time, everyone had a minimum of eight things crossed off their list. Why? When you put forth ideas and keep them ever present in the mind, we begin to do little things which cause us to "position" ourselves a bit closer toward the reality. Mark has called and looked into skydiving ~ that took place several years later. David had eagerly gone to swim practice, night after night, working diligently ~ without adults pushing him. Twice since the list, he was elected to swim in the Junior Olympics for the team representing the State of Maine.

Slowly, each of us has worked on (most sub-consciously) our list, getting closer to doing something, accomplishing others, adding new things, and even changing our minds about some original entries. So, what's the bottom line? We become believers that if we try, if we persist, if we put some effort into something... we can make it happen. That's the foundation for a "can-do" attitude. The feeling is contagious... and transferable!

There is an exercise on page 68 to help you explore this concept.

Teaching ~ Testing ~ Grading

Before the first lesson is taught, the assessment must be completed. Learning is not a guessing game ~ or at least it needn't be. When we design the form of assessment prior to teaching, we are guided by it through the lessons. We are clearly aware of what elements and ideas are important and valued. We are much more assured of keeping on track and leading discussions in productive directions.

Most importantly, we remove ourselves from the game of "Oh, it's been a few weeks. Guess I need to test them. Let's see, 50 questions = 2 points each, that will be easy to correct and should kill an entire period." Making a test after the teaching is done is unjust to the learner. In fact, why not give them the assessment up front? If we are truly interested in their learning and not the game of question/answer testing, why would we not articulate that which we felt was worth knowing?

Generating the assessment ahead of teaching creates the vision of what we expect, what is important, and what needs to be covered. It sends a message to students that you are interested in their learning above the grading process. It takes the mystery out of the teaching/learning experience. Bottom line: If you haven't made the assessment before the teaching begins ~ don't bother!

Procedures or Routines

Procedures are the rules, the patterns, the way you'd like things to be. Routines are what actually happen. Let's face it. Everyone has procedures and rules. Most spend significant time reminding people that there are rules and exactly what they are. In practice, if we are continually reminding people of our procedures (for sharpening pencils, using the pass, leaving class, etc.) then they have not become routine.

Developing a vision, articulating it, and practicing it for several weeks at the onset of a new school year can minimize reminders. Think of a combination lock. What happens if you do not follow the procedure (left 27, right 3, left 14)? It does not open. No one reminds you. No one disciplines you. You simply do it over again and again and again… until you get it right. In order for classroom procedures to become routines, you must follow the same process. First, clearly articulate the procedure. Next, practice ~ over-and-over ~ until it is routine.

Example: Getting the class's attention in five seconds or less. Tell the class the procedure: "When I want your attention, I will raise my hand and say 'Give me five.' At that time I will raise my hand and commence counting from one to five, lifting one finger with each count. When you hear me begin this, stop whatever you are doing and join me, with your hand in the air, counting aloud. At "five" I expect you to be facing me, quietly, ready for instruction." Then… practice. Have them talk and then go through the drill. Two, three or more times, even after they get it right. Do it again the second day. Do it over and over ~ especially if they forget. Articulating and repeating the procedure will cause it to become routine. You will then spend your instructional time instructing!

Celebrations, Not Rewards

We need to establish reasons to participate other than for an external reward at the end of a project. Instead of having a pizza party if the school recycles 24 tons of paper, or ice cream to the class who collects the most magazines on the drive – try celebrating the concept *up front.*

The reason we recycle has to do with conservation and preservation, respect for our environment and living things (including humans). Instead of concluding with an event, kick the project off with it! Have a special assembly with a performer who deals with the theme you are embracing. Light the fires of interest and the desired values *before the activity takes place*. We need to instill participation because it is important to do... not so as to win a contest. Create the vision of worth and sense of community. The students will rise to the occasion. Value beats food every time.

Strategy 3

Challenge Activities

CAUSE ONE TO STRETCH, GROW, RISK, & EXTEND

Challenge Activity Defined: 1. Something that is a first time occurrence; 2. Unfamiliar or potentially embarrassing; 3. Requiring one to go beyond, to be uncomfortable, to risk; 4. A demanding task which might otherwise be skirted or even avoided.

Purpose

To generate first-time activities which are unfamiliar; to require someone to go beyond previous boundaries; to cause one to be uncomfortable, to be out of their personal "comfort zone;" to compel a demanding task which would otherwise be avoided or left undone.

When we push someone to stretch, to entertain something less ordinary, less commonplace, we cause them to crash through their previous boundaries; boundaries which are typically self imposed. Once freed from former shackles, the excitement of possibilities can drive a hunger for more.

How

If our mindsets are filled with visions of failure, we are tentative about embracing the unknown. We become dulled to the humdrum of daily tasks, plodding through the hours, bored. We stop believing we can do new things. We stop believing in our ability to figure things out, to overcome hurdles, to persist beyond the obstacles before us. It looks too much like work and too little like a risk with a worthy payoff. "What's In It For Me?" yields an untenable... "Not much."

Conversely, challenges, by definition, create an atmosphere of newness; of novelty. They tax one's capabilities. When done, they become powerful stimulators and motivators. Challenge activities are essential to feelings of self esteem. When we guide another to take on a challenge (and assist as needed, to persist, to encourage or to begin again), the feeling of accomplishment builds a sense of "can do" which is transferred to other arenas.

"If you always do what you've always done, you'll always get what you've always got." If you do the same old routine, you'll likely get the same old results. If you continue to do that which generates ill feeling in your life, you'll probably continue to get the same feeling. Challenges break us out of the old syndrome and foster feelings of confidence and capability in solving problems.

In Practice

It has long been understood why groups of people from an organization will travel to remote areas to take part in outdoor challenge activities, as a team building exercise. The interdependency required to perform risks becomes a challenge for the entire group. Each situation places new or extended demands upon the participants. As people learn they can succeed where they once did not believe, they grow both personally and, if with co-workers, professionally.

One body of research suggests that teaching another person is the single best method for retaining learning. Have an employee conduct a portion of the orientation for a new hire. Teaching a portion of the procedures or other pertinent information will cause the "teacher" to refresh his/her knowledge and also feel more involved.

Doing new, *better* practices is a key to productivity. Similarly, removing the practices which have outlived their usefulness also contributes toward higher performance. Identify, by yourself or as a department, three things you've been doing that you could deliberately stop doing. Things which are no longer helpful would be good. Things which are actually perceived as impeding progress are even better.

Make a list of five adversities you (the workplace) face. Describe two ways you could react to the adversity, one toward improvement or success ~ the other despair.

Off the Wall

It's not easy taking my problems one at a time, when they refuse to get in line.

Ashleigh Brilliant

Highlights

It takes courage to push yourself to places you've never been before... to test your limits... to break through barriers. Accepting the challenges creates the basis for achievement and the exhilaration of a "can-do" attitude.

"When you play it safe, say it safe, sing it safe, paint it (or manage it) safe...

You play, say, sing, paint (and manage) the life out of it.

> The face, the voice, the music, the performance:
>
> Those are true beauty belonging to people too full of life
>
> To be afraid of making mistakes."

Dr. Gary Phillips

"All glory comes from daring to begin."

Weighing the Facts

What Greenleaf Learning Says...

Challenges create situations where we must look hard at how we perceive ourselves, how capable we believe we can be. With each new challenge comes the question of worth and competence. As our repertoire of successfully met challenges mount, our sense of self and confidence grows. As our perceptions of our own performance are enhanced, we become more willing to risk, try a new idea, or initiate constructive actions.

Providing reasonable challenges, or steps for an employee to take, are essential to our feelings of contribution and capability on the job. It is a vote of confidence. If one believes s/he can succeed (given reasonable efforts), then an effort will come. Similarly, if one believes you have "awarded" them a valued task or responsibility ~ one which exceeds prior requests and requires their extended effort ~ they can "try-out" for an enhanced status in your eyes (and in personal efficacy). Everybody wins.

Even with a history of unsuccessful events, an employee, colleague, or learner can be rejuvenated if they feel an honest respect and trust extended their way. A series of small successes will demonstrate renewed faith and motivate a person to become an active, contributing member of the team. We all want to belong ~ and need to know we make a difference!

Implementing the Process

The exercise on the next page is designed to prompt multiple ideas about areas of interest an employee or student might have. It is intended to be light hearted, soliciting anything at all which a person could want to do. The array of ideas will go from very simple, easy activities (rent a new movie release and watch it this weekend) to things which will require moderate levels of time and planning (arrange a department outing or take the family camping). Other ideas may include those desires which would require years of planning and preparation to bring about (a trip to Hawaii, getting a job which is two levels above my present one, etc.).

Work with a person to identify the things which could easily be done right away… and challenge them to maintain the list, doing at least one each week! This will build a sense of accomplishment and investment in creating a tomorrow which is a little bit more the way the person might like it to be. Then, begin thinking about the moderate activities. What would it take? Which one would be easiest? Which would be most fun? etc.

We often spend more time planning a one week vacation than we do planning elements important to the rest of our lives. A few minutes each day can build heightened awareness of one's ability to influence outcomes in their life. In time, given enough small achievements, the willingness and desire to conquer additional challenges will grow.

Though trite at first, each accomplishment serves to build a history ~ a series of "can-do" movies which are readily transferred to other circumstances. Work in the most promising arena, where success can more readily happen. Then, move to the more substantial arenas. Investing in people pays dividends ~ but you've got to keep your money in the bank!

50 Things I Want to Do **Exercise** (While I'm Alive!)

If you could do anything you wanted, whether it be simple or difficult, easy to accomplish or requiring much time and planning, what might you do? Make a list of anything that comes to mind. From the most mundane things to the elaborate… put them all down. Try not to edit your thoughts. Just jot down everything that you think of for 5-10 minutes!

1. ______
2. ______
3. ______
4. ______
5. ______
6. ______
7. ______
8. ______
9. ______
10. ______
11. ______
12. ______
13. ______
14. ______
15. ______
16. ______
17. ______
18. ______
19. ______
20. ______
21. ______
22. ______
23. ______
24. ______
25. ______
26. ______
27. ______
28. ______
29. ______
30. ______
31. ______
32. ______
33. ______
34. ______
35. ______
36. ______
37. ______
38. ______
39. ______
40. ______
41. ______
42. ______
43. ______
44. ______
45. ______
46. ______
47. ______
48. ______
49. ______
50. ______

Applications

The following ideas apply to the school, the classroom, the home, the home-school partnership, and one-on-one relationships. Embracing challenges builds esteem far more than praise can. Students need a healthy repertoire of past experiences where challenges were levied and success was theirs.

School Wide A high school principal in Seattle, on the first day of school, handed each student a paper on which to list 50 things they wanted to do in their life. He collected these lists and began connecting kids with activities they indicated they wished to do (but were either not ready for, didn't feel they could actually do, or hadn't gotten around to).

This activity helped some to make connections between their studies and some things they wished to do in their lives. Still others were challenged to accomplish several items on their list. A few were deliberately guided toward listed items as an act of demonstrating how, given a reasonable effort, these things were doable.

One group of seven outcasts, who all listed skydiving, were given lessons and then made their first jump before the entire student body. After successfully landing, their classmates congratulated them and admitted their reluctance to do the same. Each day after they entered school as "one of the seven who jumped," they began to realize that if they could tackle the challenge of skydiving, they perhaps could take on other challenges (like math, athletics or something else on their list).

Quote "When you play it safe, say it safe, sing it safe, paint it safe or manage it safe... you play, say, sing, paint and manage the life out of it."

Dr. Gary Phillips, National School Improvement Project, PO Box 1234, Issaquah, WA 948027.

20 Things List Earlier in this book," I spoke of a list of "*20 Things*"... a list of ideas or areas of interest to perhaps pursue at some point in one's life. Take a moment to compile such a list. The exercise on page 68 may be adjusted to serve as a useful template. Use it as a source of challenge activities. One by one, select an entry and begin to work on it; accomplish it, plan it, learn more about it. Keep the list visible and ever present. Share your efforts with another person ~ articulate! Use the following template as a guide.

Life Challenges Many years ago, I resigned from an Assistant Superintendent's position, due to boredom (lack of challenge). I decided to become involved in a major challenge activity every year afterward, so as not to lose sight of my aliveness. The first year's activity was to ski, as an OK-but not expert skier, Tuckerman's Ravine on Mt. Washington, in New Hampshire. I came prepared for lifts and the lodge. I discovered a 4.5 mile hike, with gear on one's back, no lodge... and no intermediate trails. One had to climb the steep ravine, find a big rock to perch upon, while managing to step into skis, and ~ chattering knees and all ~ ponder the "advanced vertical challenge" below. This was more than a challenge, it was terrifying.

It was clear that one run was going to be enough for a lifetime. Two aborted turns into the descent and I became a ball of white, whirring, entangled entertainment for the crowd of 1,000 watching below. As I picked myself up and gathered my gear, I realized it didn't matter that I had wiped out. I had skied the ravine ~ more or less. I had embraced the challenge, and (though poorly) done it.

From that day on, whenever I feel overwhelmed, I recall "Tuckerman's" and a sense of "I can figure this out" comes to me. The next year I took my two sons. They too, now recall the great challenge ~ especially when they are confronted with the difficulties of today!

Policies Like so many "official" documents, policies can be difficult to decipher. Challenge your students to rewrite school wide policies, with a twist. No word may appear twice on the new document. No "an," "the," or "and" may be used more than once. This is a literary challenge. It's amazing how writing changes. It's also interesting how understandable (and simple) the policies can become.

Cultural Have students rewrite fairy tales with various challenges: make them politically correct; update the characters to modern times; write one from the perspective of a law enforcement officer or a drug dealer; alter the story so the villain becomes the hero and vice versa. Ask students to alter the story to accommodate someone with a disability, a gift, a greed, a spy mission, or from the perspective of a teenager today.

Quote "All glory comes from daring to begin."

Teaching Research indicates the single best way to learn anything... is to teach it. One month later it is reported to be 92% effective (retention rate). Knowing this, whenever we can enlist a youth to teach something, s/he learns best. In industry, we suggest the safety violators be placed in the role of teaching new hires the safety procedures (with some supervision). The very act of being responsible for another's safety practices causes these "offenders" to pay closer attention to safety.

Similarly, cause your students (particularly those with low self-images) to explain things to others. This is not to merely give a report, but to truly assist another classmate (not just a "little kid" from a markedly lower grade) in their understanding of something. This does not have to be the subject of study. Even an unrelated topic will yield the same results.

Clearly, the act of teaching a peer is challenging to most youth. The responsibility is greater than in most situations... and for those who historically have not done well, it can be intimidating. Persist. Successful completion of such a role will have significant implications for the student. The challenge will produce long-term memory, and a more thorough understanding.

Workplace Challenge employees to identify three to five things which have outlived their usefulness, or three to five things which are not productive. Each week, select one of the items and agree among each other not to do that for the entire week. As a group effort, this will force everyone to monitor the situation ~ and, perhaps, even to come up with a replacement or alternative idea.

Sometimes, the challenges can be fun. Why not? Increasing productivity or learning is not doomed to the domain of boredom or tedium.

Activities A staff used a workshop day in an exercise to foster teambuilding and better communications. They were placed in random groups, and given identical assignments. Each group had several obstacles to overcome in order to successfully accomplish their task. Each time a new hurdle was before them, they would have to discuss, make decisions, plan, and proceed. Some challenges were physical, some academic, and some social.

Creating Mindsets ~ Developing Responsible Long-Term Behavior

ONE MOMENT PLEASE...

**Most of us have many things we would like to do before we leave this earth.
Jot down, without editing, twenty (20) things
you'd like to try ~ as fast as they come to mind...
No order, no explanation.**

1. ______
2. ______
3. ______
4. ______
5. ______
6. ______
7. ______
8. ______
9. ______
10. ______
11. ______
12. ______
13. ______
14. ______
15. ______
16. ______
17. ______
18. ______
19. ______
20. ______

Strategy 4

"AS-IF"

"Treat people 'as-if' they already are what they are capable of being...

"NOT AS THEY ARE."

"As-If" Activity Defined: The perspective of treating someone as-if they are worthwhile, capable, and productive can powerfully cause them to "try-out" for the better role. If we feel others believe in us, we tend to put forth greater effort. If we predict success, we are far more likely to achieve it. The same is true of failure.

Purpose

To foster new mindsets that prompt behaviors which are more productive for an individual.

How

When you approach people with positive expectations, they tend to call upon past experiences in which they were successful in dealing with a circumstance. Thus, they react out of possibility, rather than impossibility.

If few or no past successful experiences are available, the person will look at you almost as if to say, "Why are you asking me?" or "Have you got the right person?" Either way, treating someone "as-if" s/he is willing and able to do something suggests that you believe they truly can… a thought which may have escaped them for some time. When another adult, especially a mentor, shows faith in us, it is difficult to let them down. We welcome their confidence in us, even though we do not feel it ourselves.

It's the self-fulfilling prophecy. You find what you look for. If you believe something to be true (or possible), you begin to invest, to position yourself, to do little things which make it more possible. In time, it actually becomes more than a distant hope. It becomes real.

This is a subtle, but most powerful approach. It automatically transfers your perception of belief into the other person. It slowly becomes internalized, and in time is generated from within ~ without the external stimulus provided by you.

In Practice

One manager, in the state of Texas, introduces his workforce as "The thirty-six best workers in the State of Texas." Given enough introductions, the idea outlives its resistance and "corniness," and has been adopted by the firm as the formal introduction to each member. Repeatedly articulated, the staff now refers to themselves as "One of the 36 best workers in the state of Texas..." and they believe it!

Off the Wall

Highlights

> **"Treat people as if they were what they ought to be and you help them become what they are capable of being."**
>
> Goethe

"The leader's job is to see the Organization, not as it is... but as it can become."

Excellence can be attained if you...

- **Care more than others think is wise**
- **Risk more than others think is safe**
- **Dream more than others think is practical, and**
- **Expect more than others think is possible.**

Weighing the Facts

What Greenleaf Learning Says...

The act of treating someone "as-if" they were *already* better than they currently are (performing or being) is one that encourages another to become more of what s/he is capable of being. Success exists in every person and circumstance. Sometimes the hardest thing to do ~ is to explicitly look for it... especially when one's past experiences suggests it is unlikely.

It's like Pygmalion. <u>We tend to find what we look for</u>. If we look for shortcomings and failure, it is there. Similarly, if we look for capability, progress or success, it too, is there. We can strive to help others see more in themselves, or to accept themselves as they are. Progress will come from the gentle nudges toward improved performance.

It is far too easy to join the employee in the reality of defeat, despair or cynicism. Treating someone "as-**is**" may serve to support the very deficiency you would like to eradicate. The capacity to approach someone with an "as-**if**" perspective demands a vision of how that person might be, should they fully apply themselves.

A person's capacity to envision the very best they can be is empowered through the "as-if" action. Who would you be willing to approach, "as-if," for the next three weeks?

Implementing the Process

The activity on the following page is indicative of many such similar approaches which could be done. The first two questions deal with personal worth and esteem. They get at areas in which a person already believes they contribute... and an area in which their efforts toward growth might readily occur. Number 3 does not need to be formalized, but can be effective, if done as an entire department or company. The approach might be termed, "**Adopt-A-Person.**" It is intended to be voluntary. Those inclined to "adopt" another person need only display mild, passing interest in the individual's presence at work. The *Make Me Feel Important* principle is operative here. Simply, and briefly, notice the person. The act of being recognized (that you're even here) will send a message of "I'm important enough to be addressed." Here are a few do's and don'ts.

DO:

- Select only one person in whom you have an authentic interest
- Approach the person "as-if" s/he were already an important cog in the company, department, or organization
- Persist. This will take at least 21 consecutive days to begin to take hold. Interaction must be deliberate, not happenstance
- Change your "adoptee" at any time. Do not continue with someone if you have lost interest
- Allow more than one person to adopt the same individual
- Invite failure. Let participants know it's O.K. to let go, if it's not working.

DON'T:

- Police the activity, but encourage. Keep it low key
- Expect immediate reactions or results
- Overdo or dramatize. Be brief and unobtrusive

Adopt-A-Person Activity

Think of a student in your classroom, or a colleague at your school with whom you have been affiliated long enough to understand some of their situation. Ask him or her the following questions or try one of these approaches:

1. **Past Movie**

   In the space below, ask and note, "what are you already better at than other students or teachers etc. around here?" Record their response(s).

   ____

   ____

2. **Imagined Movie**

   In the space below, ask and note, "if you could learn to become better at something (than others), what would you like to learn to become better at?" Record their response(s).

   ____

   ____

3. **List of Comments**

   In the space to the right, invite your colleagues, others (or simply try this on your own) to:

   - Select a person; one that you really believe could do better, given a little extra attention... a constructive nudge.
   - With help from others, as needed, generate a list of comments you could make that reflect either what this person is already "good at" or "would like to become better at." List at least 10-15 items before you begin. You can add more as you go along.

   Engage this person <u>daily</u> with a very brief conversation (5-10 seconds) ~ ***no lengthy dialogue!.*** Continue this for at least three or four weeks without missing a day. If you miss a day, start over ~ counting the three or four weeks from the beginning. The practice must be uninterrupted.

   By the end of this timeframe, the person you selected will likely be discussing several ways to move forward, using their skills to achieve more in their desired area.

1. ______________________________
2. ______________________________
3. ______________________________
4. ______________________________
5. ______________________________
6. ______________________________
7. ______________________________
8. ______________________________
9. ______________________________
10. ______________________________
11. ______________________________
12. ______________________________

Applications

Below are ideas for the school, the classroom, the home, the home-school partnership and for one-on-one relationships.

Adopt-A-Kid This activity is done like a ritual (Strategy 7). Any adult can volunteer to take part. The steps are as follows:

1. An adult selects a child s/he wishes to "adopt"

2. For the next 21 days in a row (in which you are both present), the adult simply speaks to the child. It must be at a time when you are not expected or required to (i.e. not in class; but in the hall, at lunch, at beginning or dismissal time). Caution: You may not speak more than one sentence. Brevity is desired. When we speak to a child who is unaccustomed to being addressed, s/he generates resistance, "What do you want?" and "Why are you talking to me? I didn't do anything!" Whatever the situation, keep moving. Do not stop and converse. Merely speak to, or ask a question of the adoptee, with no extended interest.

The child is typically not used to being addressed, except for "school" reasons. S/he will likely have crossed eyes (Cognitive Dissonance) as you begin this exercise. In time, s/he will actually seek you out ~ without a prompt from you. When the child initiates conversation, *then* you may have an extended dialogue ~ not before.

The underlying motivation behind this approach is the MMFI concept (make me feel important). Many children (and adults) come and go from their daily routines without ever being spoken with about non-work things. All conversation centers around work related things, and is not felt to be an expression of interest in the person... as separate from the employee/student. The act of being noticed ~ as them ~ is subtle, but powerful. If you make it to the 21st day... without missing a single one... it will work!

Redirecting Resist the temptation to answer questions. When possible, redirect the inquiry to the person asking the question. Treat them as-if they can resolve their own question. "Jerry, if you were leading the expedition, what would you hope they would have considered?" "Samantha, how would this affect you?"

Procedure for Identifying "Invisible Kids" in Your School or Class

Process for Consideration

1. Post all student names (on index cards or half-sheets of paper) on a wall.
2. Give each adult or teacher about 10 blue sticker dots and ten yellow sticker dots (colors may vary).
3. Ask each person to place a blue sticker on the name of each student they know well and have a close relationship with. Then ask them to place yellow stickers on the names of students who they feel they know somewhat, but not really well. You may want to discuss each category and agree on criteria for selection in each, prior to placing the stickers. Not all 10 stickers must be used. Only place stickers on the names of students who qualify. If more stickers are needed by some teachers, that is fine... but remind them to scrutinize the criteria in identifying which students fit each category for them.
4. When all have finished placing stickers, move the student names into three groupings: those with one or more blue stickers, those with one or more yellow stickers (but no blue), and those without any stickers.
5. Ask participants what they notice about the three groups ~ characteristics, needs, etc.
6. Discuss and brainstorm what ideas could be considered to assure that all students had a blue sticker on their name.
7. Revisit the groupings twice each year to determine what changes may have taken place.

Resident Experts

Ask the students/faculty what they are really good at, perhaps even better at than anyone else in the building (in their class). Some can respond readily (past movies). Create a "Hall of Fame," in which they are featured... "Mary Bruno... Resident Expert in Algebra. If you need help in math, see Mary." Something like this, accompanied by a smiling photo, sends a message to all that Mary is really good at something.

Some do not have a repertoire of past movies which tell them they are good at much of anything. Go to the future, imagined movie. Ask them, "If you could learn to be better at something than your classmates (colleagues), what would you want to become good at?" With persistence, most will offer an idea. This is a key to what might motivate this person. Treat them as if they both want to, and are going to, act on this desire ~ be it a school related item or not. Link the person up with opportunities, places, people who can help bring this about. As the person begins to improve in this area, you now can enter them in the "Hall of Fame."

One 15 year-old indicated he was good at nothing, but interested in space travel. He was hooked up with Boeing Aircraft. Every Thursday at 10 am, he called and spoke with an employee of Boeing who had come to the school from NASA. After several weeks, he knew more about space than anyone at his school. Come science fair time ~ he proved it!

Teacher to At-Risk Student

"Melanie, what college will you be attending after graduation?" Melanie wasn't even sure about graduation, never mind college. Her mindset did not place her with the type of student who would be going on to college. Still, every day, her teacher asked a question of her which presumed she was thinking about her future and her current investment in that future (addressed her "as-if" she were going).

In time, Melanie began to look more closely at those who were slated to attend post secondary educational opportunities. She began to inquire as to what it might take. Upon graduation, she was accepted at the regional vocational college. Two years later, she graduated and started her own business.

Fostering Participation

Several years ago, a group of us were traveling in a state vehicle for a distance which would take about six hours to travel. We were largely strangers. One character in the front of the fifteen passenger van (Andre) turned around and addressed the group. "How about if we play that numbers game we used to play as kids? We have several hours of travel ahead of us. It will help pass the time, and we might get to know each other better."

Everyone looked more deeply into their book, or magazine. A few muttered, "no thanks," and we all hoped he'd go away. He persisted. "Come on. We can't read all day, and we're all going to this conference together. It will be fun," he insisted. Still, the group did not take him up on the offer. We all went back to our own personal spaces, and continued the anonymity by immersing ourselves in the materials before us.

A few moments later, Andre began calling out numbers. Out loud, so that everyone could hear the calling, he started the progression. "There's a one!" he exclaimed. Though we tried desperately to ignore him, the next shout was difficult to ward off. "Two," he said excitedly… "See the two on that sign?" A few of us could not help but to look. There it was, just as he suggested. The deliberate calling out continued. "There's a three and four!" "And five! See the five on that truck?!"

It was becoming more and more difficult to ignore the excited man in the front of the van. He kept up... as-if we were playing with him. We had not agreed to play. We had not given him permission to play with us. He simply treated the situation "as-if" we wanted to play, but were too bashful to join in.

By the time he was saying, "Ten. I see a ten!" half the riders were pointing out numbers for him, to be sure he did not miss one. A short while later, everyone was playing. In fact, six hours later, when the van arrived in the destination city, we elected to drive around in search of the magical "1,000" before we would go to the conference center.

Andre knew people enjoyed games. He also knew that we could never last six hours without talking to one another. He took charge and treated us "as-if" we were going to play. And... we did!

Quote

"I am not who I think I am. I am not who you think I am. I am who I think you think I am."

Opening Day

The administrator addressed the staff as follows: "Well, this year the bad news is the construction promised to be completed by August... ain't done. So, we'll have to put up with the dust and noise and all. They say it'll be done by November. Plan on Christmas. Good news is there's only 183 days left to school this year."

He continued, "And those textbooks you ordered... been put on hold due to central office accounting procedures ~ so, don't expect them for some time. This year is accreditation, so we'll be calling on each of you to serve on three or four useless committees, that drone on and one." As you might easily determine, he was treating the staff "as-if" everything was one big discouragement, if not hopeless. If you treat people as worthy, they act worthy. If you treat them as downtrodden, they will act downtrodden.

Our approach to a class, a student, a spouse, etc. will have a tremendous effect upon how they respond. Treat them as-if they are capable and, in time, they will act capable. Treat them as ding-a-lings... and that's probably what you'll get.

Suggestive Reasoning

Instead of asking someone, "Are you going?" ask "When are you going?" The latter implies that they are, and that the only thing left to do is to determine when. Instead of asking, "Have you thought about post-secondary schooling?" ask "If you went to XYZ Institute, what would you study?" Instead of asking, "Have you spoken with Mr. Smith about this?" ask "What did Mr. Smith say when you spoke with him?"

The practice of treating a person as-if s/he has done, or is going to do something suggests you know they have the ability and intention of following through.

Problem Solving

Too often, something happens and an adult comes on the scene and takes over. We see something wrong, a mistake, an accident, etc. We step in to remedy the situation as quickly as possible. When you think about it, this renders adults as empowered problem solvers, and youth as lowly problem creators.

Try this, a la Barbara Colorosa. Something unfortunate happens (Harold is accidentally bumped and drops his lunch tray). Do not fix the situation. Instead, ask the two students (Harold and the "bumper"), "What is the problem?" Be sure, however obvious, that you have them define the problem. Harold could say the problem was that Chris bumped him. The real problem is that there is food on the floor.

Once defined, ask the two co-owners of the issue, "What do you need to do to solve the problem?" Let them discuss the matter and come up with a solution. If unreasonable, they return to discussion to re-think the remedy. If reasonable, help them to carry out their plan. This way, the students are treated as-if they can resolve their own issues, without relying upon an adult to come up with the appropriate course of action. This way, the skill of problem solving is transferable. It is now "owned" by the student(s), in place of a more dependent status.

Compliments

Rather than ask people to deliver compliments, empower and expect it of them. Determine something specific and sincere you wish to compliment someone on. Pay them the compliment in terms of a certificate or ribbon, handing them two. One is for them. The second one is for them to pass on, to compliment someone else. Approach them as-if they will, as-if they want to. Not surprisingly, most will.

Strategy 5

Paradoxical Inventions

Health... Nutrition... Hygiene... Health... Nutrition...

IN ORDER TO UNDERSTAND HOW TO IMPROVE THINGS, first determine how to make them worse.

Paradoxical Intentions Defined: 1. Instead of reacting in a direct, rational manner, consider an approach which is 180° from conventional logic; 2. Before making efforts to improve the circumstances, first take a look at what it would take to make things even worse than they already are. For Example: "What could you do, that is not already being done, that would make this situation more dismal than it currently is?"

Purpose

To foster critical thinking; to cause the person or class to think about what they are doing/have done/have said in a new way; to view something from an entirely different angle; to cause one to examine the logic or rationale behind traditional or conventional thinking; to break automatic responses and give rise to concerted thought.

How

Instead of reacting in a manner that is expected, consider an approach which is 180 degrees from that commonly done. Therefore, before you try to direct someone toward a suitable, appropriate outcome ~ first take a step back, pause, and consider another means of engaging the learner.

Sidestep the obvious dialogue, and engage in discussion surrounding a totally opposite reaction or course of action. Suggest that the individual or group consider the ramifications of a radically different strategy. The fall-out from such an approach is to create critical thinking about what made the initial request important in the first place. What is the underlying value beneath the comment which has been put forth? Is it really valid? Why?

By causing someone to reconsider... or to at least carefully consider reasons "to" and reasons "not-to..." they engage in a thought process which can dislodge callous remarks or actions. You may even be able to avoid acting out of an authority role. Reactions from us which are completely "out of left field" can help one double back and consider the merits of the action of request. It is far more important that the learner comes to understand an alternative "way to be," than to be told what to do. The former teaches him/her to fish; the latter merely feeds him/her fish.

In Practice

- Manager: "To be more oppressive, what could I do that I haven't already been doing?"
- Anyone: "If we could choose something to fail at, what would be the best practice to fall short on achieving?"
- Supervisor: "If you didn't want to improve on the job, what could you do to insure that things remained the same?"
- Project Leader: Give inaccurate information to your "top flight" people while offering the correct material to the laggards. The process deliberately sets up those who typically contribute less to lead the "high fliers." The discussion and outcomes may produce better thinking along the way ~ even superior results!
- Co-Worker: "One of my fellow workers came to work and daily made life miserable for me. One day I requested that he help with an *after work* project to assist a friend of mine who lived in his neighborhood. The issues at work cleared up instantaneously!"

Off the Wall

"Every now and then I do something my bosses want me to do...

just to keep them on their toes!"

Highlights

The paradox asks us to abandon logical, rational, cause-effect thinking, and to expose our repeated actions, which are unwittingly contributing to our failures.

Five Ways to Encourage Your Employees to Hate Their Jobs.

1. Talk *to* your employees, not *with* them, and never listen.
2. Put your employees off when they ask "why," and tell them, "Because I said so."
3. Lead your employees to believe that you are perfect and infallible.
4. Always expect the worst and never give them the benefit of the doubt.
5. Don't *ever* trust them.

Weighing the Facts

What Greenleaf Learning Says...

The paradox of having reactions be exactly opposite what is expected causes us to interact with internal "mindsets." As we engage our stored or anticipated movies, we quickly note the dissonance between what has occurred and what might have been. This very action causes us to do a double take ~ to consider more fully our action or request. The circumstances surrounding our thinking are questioned, promoting more perspectives. This activity alone can cause one to re-think... or at least to reconstruct possible options. Often, this is enough to prompt other points of view.

So many times we become victims of habit. We conduct our lives out of consistent patterns which have been successful ~ or at least acceptable ~ in our past. And why wouldn't we? Now and then we maintain a focus or a position which has outlived its usefulness. Presenting a paradox to the circumstance forces the question, "Is this the only way that makes sense?" Once jarred, many possibilities that may once have formally been obscure become options.

There is a different feel to using the paradoxical intention from more common approaches. "So... what could *you* do, that you are not already doing... to cause your staff to be even ***less*** productive than they already are?"

Implementing the Process

The exercise on the next page is intended to cause people to consider alternatives which are, at first blush, directly opposite their common practice. Start by identifying a situation which is problematic or perpetual. Before seeking solutions, we gain as much by knowing what ***NOT*** to do... as we do in working to resolve. Sometimes, removing the barriers can promote more efficient practices than searching for ways to improve what is happening ever will.

Once you have identified the situation arena, list at least three things you personally could do to cause detriment or failure. Be sincere and realistic as to things you actually might purposefully, or inadvertently do.

Next, list three things someone "above" you in the organizational ladder might do which would cause a worsened situation, or failure. Go on and fill in three things others (peers, customers, vendors, etc.) could do to create a more dismal circumstance.

At this point, it should be simple to see all that could go wrong. Take a moment to determine what you could do to avert each of the listed disasters to your cause. Being aware, and then planning for adversities can help to avoid them altogether. Based on what could go wrong... do you now have a few ideas about how to improve the situation?

"We are continually faced by great opportunities brilliantly disguised as insoluble problems."

Plan a Failure Exercise ~ The Paradoxical Intention

Identify a Situation or Circumstance	

CREATING Failure	**BUILDING Success**
What 3 things can YOU do to make failure more likely?	What 3 things can YOU do to make success more likely?
1.	1.
2.	2.
3.	3.

What 3 things can a PARENT or TEACHER do to make failure more likely for you?	What 3 things can THEY do to make success more likely for you?
1.	1.
2.	2.
3.	3.

What 3 things can FRIENDS or SCHOOLMATES do to make failure more likely for you?	What 3 things can THEY do to make success more likely for you?
1.	1.
2.	2.
3.	3.

Applications

The following apply to the school, the classroom, the home, the home-school partnership, and to one-on-one relationships.

Mix-Up Try giving correct information to those in the class who tend more to struggle, and incorrect or inadequate information to those who pick things up quite easily. Then, conduct a discussion as usual. Watch or listen carefully to the reactions and ideas unfold, as the class works through possibilities and ideas. The entire process may generate better thinking, and a more thorough dialogue.

Ask "If you were deliberately going to make this a worse place than it already is, what would you do to accomplish this?" Keep a record of the ideas. When someone actually does one of them… they have done something ~ by their own admission ~ which is not in their best interest.

Getting the Negative Out of the Way A corporate leader brought all the company managers into the conference room to discuss a new idea ~ a new strategy for approaching marketing. First, the group was asked to take turns as they went around the table, and for each to indicate what was wrong; what wouldn't work with respect to the idea. After they had all taken a turn indicating what was wrong with the approach, they were then asked to go around the room one more time and say one thing which might work, could work, or would be good. By the end of the second round, the room was clamoring with excitement about the prospects.

To a Complaining Student, Teacher, or Person "As bad as things are around here, what could you do to make them even worse?" (This quickly points out the behavior in which the person has been engaged. It also suggests s/he has the opportunity to impact the situation ~ by doing things to make it either better or worse ~ "empowerment.")

5 Years from Now Ask students to do a mind map or cluster of the school; how they feel, how they see it, etc. When completed, ask them to respond to the questions: "Where will you be five years from now if you quit school? Where will you be if you don't?"

Parent to Adolescent Following a Negative Remark from an Adolescent

"This is just great! As an adolescent your purpose is to be difficult, antagonistic, and to find fault. I'm delighted to see you are doing your job well. Thank you!"

This acknowledges the role of adolescence; to test the waters, to see if they can function on their own ~ without the adult to guide them. Think about it; teenagers need to find out how independent they are, how capable they will be without their lifelong protectorate (you). They are supposed to explore ways to build self-reliance. Though their actions are not always desired by adults, they have a purpose (this is not to excuse outright rudeness and inappropriate acts).

By side-stepping the emotion of the affront, you are better able to remain clear headed. You also avoid letting the "personal" nature of the commentary get under your skin. In essence, it takes some of the wind out of their sails ~ and keeps you in the driver's seat!

Exercise

"Plan a Failure." Have a person or group complete the exercise on page 86 of this book. Basically, you are asking people to identify a situation in their life (home, school, work, or relationship). Next, they will develop three perspectives on the situation: their own; that from a person in authority over them; and that from their peers. Ask them to list three things which could be done to insure it fail/get worse (three for each perspective).

The very creation of such a list points out that success and failure are the results of actions that people do... and don't do. They are empowered to make an effort ~ or to place fate in the hands of others. While they cannot control all factors in their lives, they can control that which they do ~ which just might affect some other things.

The exercise also points out potential roadblocks, challenges, and things to consider in approaching the situation.

Anyone to Teachers in the Faculty Lounge, Complaining

"As bad as things sound, what's keeping you from becoming cynical?" The question suggests that crossing the line to cynicism might already have taken place, and puts the complainers on notice that they are not in problem solving mode, but engrossed in a behavior which can only perpetuate their condition.

"As bad as things are right now, what could you do to make them worse?"

Adult to Youth, Among Friends

At the dinner table (other settings are also applicable), with your son or daughter and a friend of his/hers ask, "Janet, I know your mother is about the same age as I am. My daughter, Annie, is always complaining about my parenting style; what I do wrong, etc. I'm sure your mother does a much better job of it than I do… so could you help me out? Can you give me some ideas on how to be a better parent for Annie?"

Clearly, to put a "friend" in such a position is totally intolerable. However, the approach suggests an interest in becoming better… an interest in taking the criticisms seriously. It also lets both young people know you are willing to listen ~ AND to take them at their word. Thus, if they are to complain about something, they are also going to be held accountable for producing reasonable alternatives, ideas, and solutions.

Give it a try. Your son/daughter will undoubtedly be upset with you for such an outlandish act. However, they won't long miss the implications!

Parent, after Being Ridiculed by a Youth

"It's my job to be dumb, out-dated, wear funny clothes, drive a junky car, listen to lousy music, and inflict pain upon you in the form of curfews and limitations. Thanks for letting me know I am doing my job."

It's OK for young people to see us as "out of touch." Remember a few years ago, when you were the one who was oppressed? Adults are supposed to guide… and youth are supposed to object. It's a simple law of nature. Roll with it. Admit it, and you're halfway there. Fight it… and you wage an unwinnable war. Choose your battles. Save them for the really important issues. The rest of the stuff is usually a harmless testing of the waters. Our job is to keep the ship afloat… not to flatten the seas.

Student or Child Having a Bad Day

List all the things wrong with this school, class, or home (whatever the source of frustration). Now, create a list of what a very capable, bright person would do to make it better.

The act of putting oneself in another's shoes… especially the shoes of another who is admired for his/her capabilities, allows us to put our burdensome circumstance aside, and to utilize the best of what we know… the best of who we can be. Identifying what is "wrong" is as important as finding a solution. Solutions to non-problems are not solutions at all. Determining options for making it better provides ideas for what each of us can do to orchestrate our lives toward desired outcomes.

Strategy 6

The Virtue of Vulnerability

MAKE YOURSELF VULNERABLE TO OTHERS

1. Become emotionally engaged
2. More authentic
   a. Real
   b. Believable
   c. Humane
3. Explore workplace climate
   a. Dominant emotion
   b. Missing emotion

Virtue of Vulnerability Defined: 1. The act of putting oneself in a vulnerable position; 2. Disclosure; 3. Admitting error, mistake, or failure; 4. Recognizing one is not always good at something; 5. Confronting a fear or unwanted emotion by openly sharing it with others.

Purpose

To display authenticity; to allow others to see you as a real person, with feelings and questions and even a few insecurities; to let others know you don't have all the answers; to permit your shortcomings to show; to admit you are sometimes unsure, and sometimes in need of support.

How

In many ways, adults do not allow themselves to have the same experiences as the youth about them. We attend similar events, even orchestrate them. However, through the course of the experiences, we seem to automatically take charge, make decisions, or direct or organize some facets of the experiences. In part, this is our role, our task, our responsibility.

This is not to suggest we become "buddies" with our children or our students. This would not be in their best interest. They depend upon us to show support, and a "sense of knowing" in many situations. The younger the child, the more they need to know they are safe, and protected from harm.

Just the same, it warms the heart of youngsters to know that we too, are human. While they do not want us to be weak, a demonstration of vulnerability makes the transition to adulthood more possible ~ especially to the self-doubting mind. There are many ways we can allow others to witness our shortcomings and uncertainties. These are expressed in the applications that follow.

Do not mistake vulnerability for weakness. Nobody wants their leader, their guide, to be incompetent. We simply want to know a real person, with feelings just like ours, with experiences in their past ~ even present ~ that parallel some of what we are going through. It brings us all a little closer, a little more willing to work together, to consider an idea, and to understand.

In Practice

A manager of a technology business regularly exercises vulnerability when she puts herself in the role of the learner with her staff. They see her in a role where she knows less about the software than they do. This also places them in the position of teacher, which enhances their understanding of the products they work with. Both the manager and the employees win... and the potential for better service to customers is heightened.

The CEO of a major firm would regularly admit to the workers that he did not understand an issue fully, and needed explanation. As a result, people felt more at ease with "not knowing" everything, and the process of learning was encouraged. Making mistakes was accepted as part of the process of getting from where they were to a desired place. The CEO was viewed as approachable, and issues were brought to him that otherwise may have been buried several layers beneath him.

"Shame is in not admitting your ignorance."

Clifford White, 1986

Off the Wall

Highlights

"Failure is an essential and inevitable component of learning and the transition to [superior performance]."

Dr. Gary Phillips

It's not enough to learn the truth
unless I learn enough to live it.

It's not enough to join the crowd.

To be acknowledged and accepted.

I must be true to my ideals
even if I am excluded and rejected.

It's not enough to know what's right
unless I'm strong enough to do it.

It's not enough to reach for love
unless I care enough to give it.

It's not enough to have a dream
unless I'm willing to pursue it.

From "What's a Parent to Do?"
Dr. Gary Phillips

Weighing the Facts

What Greenleaf Learning Says...

When we must be invincible, all-knowing or "right," we place a heavy burden upon ourselves to continue to know what's best in all situations. Inadvertently, this also denies others the opportunity to learn through mistakes. Letting others see that we all are constantly learning, that we too, are interested in improvement, not just the final success ~ then we encourage growth and learning.

Being vulnerable does not mean we are laying ourselves down to be taken advantage of, or to be trodden over. Not at all. It means we improve better as a team than as islands of independence. Certainly, we each have areas of expertise which need to be shared, but often we have a void ~ a blind spot that others can help us with ~ if we establish a relationship which supports vulnerability, rather than ridicules it.

Many fear letting others know that they are not sure about something. The result is that we have an employee or colleague who proceeds, with a client or parent or on a project, with less than adequate information or skill. This places the organization in a vulnerable position of losing the faith of the parent, or community, or student. "Vulnerability begins at home," might be a good approach to promoting internal growth and competence. After all, building a "can-do" **team** is the best way to insure success. No one does it alone for very long. Your constituency deserves the best you can offer. Vulnerability at chosen moments makes you less so at the right moments!

Implementing the Process

The next page employs a very basic activity which can yield some powerful results. Its approach is toward the feelings... not the acts which accompany them. Be sure to avoid listing or stating activities or behaviors in the top portion of this exercise.

Begin with the first list. What is the prevailing emotion in your workplace? What emotion comes to mind most often when people are asked how they feel about their work? What emotion would people say is lacking, that they wish they felt more often while in the workplace? What would be appropriate? Desired? Cause greater work performance?

Collate (anonymously) the five dominant and three missing emotions in your situation. Are there some in common among all? These might be a good place to start. It is likely that, while the emotion may be the same, the stimulus will differ. That's why you need to focus upon the actual feeling, to be sure to build in supports. If negative, build small, minor practices which can serve to diminish the frequency of occurrence. The final list on the bottom half of the next page will address this.

Once the data is known to all, you can begin putting the ideas into action. Public statements will serve to make everyone aware of the serious intent to support and/or remedy the climate of the workplace. Be sure to build in rituals which review, examine, and perpetuate the smallest of activities, to sustain the desired outcomes. If the leader is willing to be vulnerable, and to place his/her stated intentions in written, public format ~ then others will be more likely to put forth effort as well. While this is deliberate and a little corny, a fun time can be made of it ~ as the culture of the workplace shifts, people will have contributed to the change, and feel a part of molding what takes place.

Workplace Emotions ~ Putting Ourselves On Notice

DOMINANT Emotions	**DEVELOPING Emotions**
List Your Five Most Dominant Emotions at Work (in this classroom, not necessarily the strongest ever, but the most prevalent):	List the three kinds of emotions you would like to feel more often at work (in this classroom):
1.	1.
2.	2.
3.	3.
4.	4.
5.	5.

If we were to do one small thing which would cause a more desired emotion to be present and a negative or dominant one to be reduced, what would we do? List some ideas.

1. ______
2. ______
3. ______
4. ______

Now, select one which everyone thinks they can do and place it in a visible place which clearly states the agreed upon activity(ies) or outcomes. There are many ways to articulate the desired goals. One, a public sign, is illustrated below.

"As good a ____________ (teacher, student, leader) as I already am... I am about to become even better, with your help.

I have a plan for improvement. I am going to begin to do more of ______________________________ (missing emotion activity) and less of ______________________ (negative/dominant emotion/activity).

I will need your input regularly as to how I'm doing."

Applications

The following ideas are for the school, the classroom, the home, the home-school partnership, and for one-on-one relationships.

Rotating Roles

Two teachers were team teaching a high school class on public speaking and communications. The course was organized such that every other class was a simulated business meeting, with one in charge, one or two making formal presentations, still others carrying out various roles of the interactive scenario. Students were put in a rotation schedule, so that each would have an opportunity to conduct each role.

As an act of vulnerability, the two teachers placed themselves in the rotation and had to take an active part, actually doing the same work as the students. They were even subject to the same evaluative criteria as the rest of the class!

Spelling

A fifth grade teacher assigned students a new list of spelling words each week. At the same time (usually Monday), she had the students go through the dictionary and find ten words SHE did not know. At the end of the week the students took their test, as usual.

After the students completed their test, they gave the teacher hers! She was placed in the same position as the students ~ vulnerable to not knowing, and to not doing well. In fact, during some weeks the teacher only had four correct answers. However, as the students would freely offer, they were working hard to help her!

Shared Responsibility

A teacher has developed a system of homework collection, for days when she is absent. A schedule is developed as to who will be responsible on the next day this occurs. One student, at the end of the normal class time, will collect all work which is due. If any work is incomplete or not done, the student in charge will determine what will happen (turn it in to him/her the next morning or lose 10% of the grade, etc).

Students are careful to meter out reasonable consequences, as the next time it may be they who have unfinished work. In the end, the teacher does not collect this work ~ it all passes through the hands of the student in charge.

Activities

During a special time for activities called "Intercession" at one school, students K-12 are involved in elective activities for three days... right along with the staff.

One group learned to do country music line dances. As the instructor led them in various steps, the adults learned them right along side the students.

Another group designed and constructed CO2 racecars. Each teacher also constructed and raced their car against the field. In the end, a student's car won the entire derby.

Still others were involved in the creation of a movie video. With both acting scenes and music creations, staff and students alike were involved in every aspect of the video development. It was delightful to see the tape played before student groups ~ and to hear the commentary, as people of all ages interacted on the "silver screen."

Sharing Feelings Instead of Thoughts

One way to be vulnerable is to simply share your feelings with the class. In lieu of the comments which typically come from our roles as responsible leaders, stop now and then and share: who you are; what you're feeling ~ not just what you're thinking. Students respond well to this.

"Who You Are" *before* "Who Are You"

A principal was proud to announce he had learned the names of every student in the K-5 school ~ all 500+ of them. He had worked hard to get to know them as best he could. This is certainly commendable... but only half the equation.

The other question is, "How well do the students know who you are?" It is when we share who we are that students respond most. Getting to know them is essential; letting them get to know us ~ is an honor. They feel special when we share ourselves with them.

So... the questions: "Is your school/classroom a reflection of you?" "Do you have 'personality' bulletin boards with such items as your report card when you were in that grade? Songs you listened to when you were their age? What was your favorite food, color, animal, activity? Something you're really good at, a hobby, a special interest?"

Stump the Teacher A middle school science teacher had a weekly "quiz time," in which the students asked any science related question of him, and he had to answer (reversed roles). If he was unable to respond, students were given five minutes of extra recess/study time. The catch: Each question to which he could not reply adequately was assigned to groups of students as their homework for that night! Even knowing this, they worked diligently to find questions he could not answer.

Best/Worst At the beginning of the year, one instructor asked two simple questions of each class:

1. "Think of the best teacher you ever had. What are the characteristics of him/her that made him/her the best for you?"
2. "Now think of the worst teacher you ever had. What characteristics made him/her this way?"

The responses are the same for all of us. No surprises. The lists create a powerful document containing what the learners believe, by self-declaration, needs to both happen ~ and NOT happen, if the class is to be productive and enjoyable.

This puts the teacher and students "on notice" as to what behaviors are desired for optimal learning. The teacher is now on public notice as to what things s/he must do in order to be "good." Similarly, the students are also subject to the very same standards and expectations ~ to be the best learners they can be.

Group Emotions On an anonymous index card, have the staff write the five dominant emotions they feel while at school (not necessarily the most intense emotions, but those felt most often). Then, have them write the three missing emotions (ones they would like to feel more often).

A simple collating of this data will usually yield "dominant" negative emotions which all have in common. There are also likely to be common "missing" emotions as well. The task is to replace the negative ones with the desired, missing ones. As a collective group, decide what you will each do when another exhibits the unwanted dominant emotions ~ that will serve to support the desired, missing ones. In a short period of time you will see a noticeable difference in attitudes and feelings.

SECTION FOUR

Introduction to the Eight Activities for Working With Young People

Each of the following eight activities is based upon the Four Foundation Mindsets of how esteem and accomplishment are achieved. These four "principles" are reviewed in the text below. The contents of this section include two activities for each of the four mindsets.

The first page of each activity is analogical. This means, its intent is to capture the feeling that accompanies the idea... the essence of what is being presented. After this is "**Planting the Seeds**," which provides directions for the "**Sculpting the Image**" exercise that follows. The activities are designed to address the overall concept with participants (students/others). The exercises may be adjusted or used as-is with individuals or with a group of people. The next components, "**What The Experts Say**," "**Highlights**," and "**Funny Bones**," offer some alternative viewpoints, approaches, and formats for broader perspective. "**From the Sidelines**," puts forth a related poem or quote. Concluding commentary about the activity, "**Weighing the Facts: What Greenleaf Learning Says**" is a bottom line with respect to this component.

The following pages are designed to provide a few examples of activities for consideration in working with youth and adults. Certainly, each will require modification for the intended purpose and for the age of the learner(s). All are grounded in the four foundation mindsets for motivation, esteem, and achievement.

Foundation #1 *I Am Capable*

Our behavior is largely dictated by how we feel. "If I *feel* capable, I *act* capable." "If I feel terrible, I act terrible." The movie we play inside our head has a dramatic impact upon how we choose to approach a situation. People who feel positive and confident about their abilities are far more apt to act in constructive ways. We need to help others understand how they contribute toward their own worth, as well as the worth of others.

Foundation #2 *Today Connects With Tomorrow*

Each of us is more motivated into action when we believe our efforts today are connected with potential benefits of tomorrow. While we cannot (and should not) provide guarantees, each of us needs to believe that if we invest in the task before us, two things are probable:

a). given reasonable effort, we can succeed

b). the outcome will be valued (importantly, by me ~ but perhaps by others, too).

We are far more likely to put forth energy if we understand how today's investment connects with tomorrow's desired outcome.

Foundation #3 *I Make A Difference*

If we believe a difference is made when we show up... we matter. All of us want to count for something. Still, we question our worth, often. When we help another to see how they really do impact their environment and/or those about them, their motivation to continue, to contribute and to get involved is heightened. We all need a sense of purpose about our efforts. This provides the meaning in our lives.

Foundation #4 *Someone Believes in Me*

Mentorship. We all have those important people in our lives, the ones who provided the support and encouragement when times were tough. At every age we have difficult moments. We all need that special person who invests in our abilities, our worth, our dreams. We need the "you can do it, I believe in you, you're going to make it, I won't give up on you" comments to bolster us through the trying times. Given this, many who would not have otherwise persisted, make it!

Activity 1 : Celebrate Improvements

WE TEND TO FIND WHAT WE LOOK FOR

Planting the Seeds

Foundation Mindset #1
I Am Capable

The process outlined here is designed to help you focus on a very small piece of success. Few of us "fall" into successful outcomes without the effort and diligence of hard work and persistence. Each decision to "*make something work*" is based upon your will to find the tiniest evidence of progress... and build upon it.

Think of a desired outcome or event that you would like to have occur. Write it in the first box on the next page. Now, being careful not to "bite off too much at a time," what might be a reasonable effort or activity that would bring you noticeably closer to accomplishing your goal? Not everything goes as planned, so consider in the area below: What might be considered improvement... even of the tiniest amount? Be sure to write it down ~ even if it seems insignificant.

The Important Part

If a reasonable (or even slight portion of a) step occurs, how will you (or others) recognize the progress? Commensurate with the level of success thus far, what **will** you do to acknowledge the difference you have made?

If we wait until the entire project is done before recognizing progress, motivation to continue will be jeopardized. Similarly, if we insist that perfection (or even completion) be reached before acknowledging progress, our need to feel accomplishment will go untended. ***We find what we look for.*** You can look for total completion and always see the unfinished parts... or you can look for progress and champion the process along the way.

Sculpting the Image ~ Finding What You Look For

We All Need Reasons, and... We Find What We Look For

- Focusing on annoying behavior... gets us annoyed.
- Looking for small improvements... benefits encouragement.

Celebrate Each Step... or the Journey May Never End!

Identify an Activity, Result, or Behavior

REASONABLE Step	**EVIDENCE of Success**
A Reasonable Step Toward Accomplishment...	The Tiniest Evidence of Improvement Might Be...

If the above improvements are made, what can I/we do to acknowledge or support further efforts?

Accomplishment Celebration Strategy	Evidence Celebration Strategy

What The Experts Say

"Strategies for improvements cause students to look at the situation in a different emotional stance than they did before... if a student (child) gets better, who knows? Who cares? And how is this improvement acknowledged, analyzed, shared, and rewarded? We find what we look for...

1. Look for improvement, not perfection.
2. Acknowledge indicators of improvement.
3. Celebrate quality performance and efforts at improvement.

If we do not acknowledge and analyze our successes, we are doomed to repeat our failures. Above all, what is important in my classroom? Improvement is at least one definable response."

Dr. Gary Phillips

"Regardless of the method used, we need to let every student know we have structured the assignment for success and we believe students can do them."

Barbara Coloroso

Highlights

1. What gets tended, gets done.
2. Looking for and recognizing improvement prior to completion inspires. The glass is thus half full, rather than half empty.
3. Small bits are easier to do than large hunks. They also tend to get done.

Funny Bones

School Improvement Chain Letter

Simply send a copy of this letter to six (6) other schools that are tired of their principals. Then bundle up your principal and send him/her to the school at the top of the list. Add the name of your school to the bottom of the list.

In one week you will receive 16,436 principals. One of them should be a dandy. Believe this... one school broke the chain letter and got its own principal back!

From the Sideline

I Celebrate Children

I celebrate children

> Who laugh out loud
> Who walk in the mud and dawdle in the puddles
> Who put chocolate fingers anywhere
> Who like to be tickled
> Who scribble in church
> Who whisper in loud voices
> Who sing in louder voices
> Who run ~ and laugh when they fall
> Who cry at the top of their lungs
> Who cover themselves with Band-Aids
> Who squeeze the toothpaste all over the bathroom
> Who slurp their soup
> Who chew cough drops
> Who ask questions
> Who give us sticky, paste-covered creations
> Who want their pictures taken
> Who don't use their napkins
> Who bury their goldfish, sleep with the dog, scream at their best friends
> Who hug us in a hurry and rush outside without their hate.

I celebrate children who are so busy living they don't have time for our hang-ups.

I celebrate adults who are as little children.

Ann Weems

Weighing the Facts

What Greenleaf Learning Says...

When we go looking... we are much more apt to see what our minds are looking for than anything else that happens. To this end, we do typically find what we look for. Look for good and you'll find it ~ even in a most difficult child or situation. Look for what's wrong and that too, will present itself. What we sincerely would like to see, if given the choice, may be a better guide for improvement than what we actually find before us on a daily basis.

It is easy to see problems. It is also easy to see what works. We are accustomed to commenting on how things might be made better. We are not so accustomed to making a similar effort to mention what goes well. Either way, it boils down to perception and expectation. What we sincerely hope for prevails.

The "movies" we play inside our heads will impact our behaviors ~ and our disposition toward an issue. If we do not believe we (or another) can achieve a certain task without a constant struggle, we'll have a tendency to look for the stumbling stones. If we are confident an outcome will happen, we seek glimpses at the indicators of progress... and find them! It becomes a self-fulfilling prophecy in many ways. We can **draw attention to that which will help** construct desired results... or we can plant the seeds of discouraging possibilities.

We all do better with encouragement. Why not "find" what's **right**... and go from there. All involved will prosper and have better dispositions along the way!

Activity 2 : Don't Be Afraid to Fail

R.I.P.

From This Day Forward,

The __________ Day

Of __________, 20_____

Let It Be Known That

____

Did Not Make It At

______________________.

LETTING GO OF FAILURE

"We Can Learn More From Mistakes Than Success"

Planting the Seeds

Foundation Mindset #1
I Am Capable

Often, we realize the benefits of allowing ourselves to accept our failures and to continue on with our lives. The difficult part is the "letting go."

The exercise on the following page serves several purposes.

1. Writing our failures on paper helps us to admit that this is something we cannot do (acceptance).
2. Sharing our failures helps us to work through discouraging feelings.
3. Physically discarding something is a symbolic act that helps us mentally and emotionally "Bury the Dead."

Just as we throw away things that are no longer useful in our everyday lives, we can also throw away our personal shortcomings. Once we remove this burden from our backs, we are free to engage in more constructive behaviors. Failure is an important part of our successes in life. Embrace it as not only inevitable, but necessary.

Sculpting the Image ~ Bury The Dead

The Process of Accepting Shortcomings

Describe the Failure

What caused my failure? ______________________________

What have I learned by this? ______________________________

There are many ways to discard unwanted items or unproductive emotions.

List any 3 things you have thrown out or discarded this month.

Activity

Choose one or more.

1. Write your current failure on 3 pieces of paper. Discard each paper in the same manner as you discarded 3 items this month.
2. Mail a copy of your failure to each of 3 friends who can support your failure's funeral... and have them agree to stop you, if you bring it up again!
3. Create a "mock casket." Have a ceremony with at least one other person present. Say your good-byes and bury the issue... for good!

What The Experts Say

"Failure is an essential and inevitable component of learning and the transition to adulthood. A nurturing attitude about confronting fears and willingly engaging in challenge activities encourages youth to realize their potential.

Dr. Gary Phillips

Throughout history, successful men and women have redefined failure as a stepping-stone to a greater success. Hyatt has a favorite adage... "Success is the ability to go from failure to failure without loss of enthusiasm."

M. Rozek

Highlights

1. Failure is a natural part of life.
2. What we choose to let go of determines what we keep.
3. Embracing failure allows us to accept it and then move on.

Funny Bones

"If the horse you're riding dies...
it's probably a good time to dismount."

From the Sideline

Let Go...

To "let go" does not mean to stop caring, it means I can't do it for someone else.

To "let go" is not to enable, but to allow learning from natural consequences.

To "let go" is not to try to change or blame another, it's to make the most of myself.

To "let go" is not to care for, but to care about.

To "let go" is not to fix, but to be supportive.

To "let go" is not to deny, but to accept.

To "let go" is not to nag, scold, or argue, but instead to search out my own shortcomings and correct them.

To "let go" is not to adjust everything to my desires but to take each day as it comes, and cherish myself in it.

To "let go" is not to criticize and regulate anyone, but to try to become what I dream I can be.

To "let go" is to not regret the past, but to grow and live for the future.

To "let go" is to fear less, and love more.

Weighing the Facts

What Greenleaf Learning Says...

Each day brings opportunity. Success and failure are part and parcel of the choices we make. Sometimes, our decisions result in accomplishment and joy. Sometimes, we fall short in disappointment.

Trying again and in other ways is a sure way to overcome short term setbacks. We need to pursue our desires to fulfillment. However, when repeated efforts do not bring us closer, and do not leave us with hope... discouragement may prevail. Beating ourselves down, or constantly proclaiming our inability to do something is seldom helpful.

Instead, "let go." Separate your personal worth and value from the activity, and take on a more promising task or approach.

It is when we dwell only and intensely on our failures that we harm ourselves and even those we care about. The key is not to focus on those issues that impede success, but to "bury them," and to focus on those things we do well. Success will follow.

Failure is a necessity of life, and as such is unavoidable. Facing and embracing failure may be your first step toward success.

Activity 3 : Developing Identity, Self Worth. Who Am I ?

"IT IS NOT WHO YOU ARE,

but that you are, which counts."

Planting the Seeds

Foundation Mindset #2
Today Connects With
Tomorrow

Who we are is reflected in what we do... and don't do. The activity on the following page is designed to draw attention to things we have already chosen to do, summarizing with a choice to affect our tomorrow.

The conscious awareness of our acts gives us a snapshot of who we have been. Our words and actions mirror the internal thoughts and feelings which guide us. Reflecting upon what we have done and how we feel about that is a vital part of selecting the next step.

Conduct the activity for a week's time or for a single day. Accomplishment and regret are possible in everything we do. It is important to know where we stand... and even more so to know where we're headed.

Sculpting the Image ~ Self Worth

Describe 3 Things You Have Done and Feel Good About

1.

2.

3.

Something that I wish I hadn't done or said.

What are you willing to do... TODAY, to make tomorrow a little bit more the way you would like it to be?

1.

2.

3.

What The Experts Say

"[We all have] the need to be a unique person; to be noticed and recognized as special. [This need is] expressed in dress, walk, talk, word choice, hobbies, interests, beliefs, etc. [It] suffers when comparisons are made; feelings are rejected or minimized; judgments are voiced [and] when the person is ignored or lumped in with others... you can help a child enhance his/her uniqueness by:

1. Communicating acceptance of them just the way they are
2. Increasing their opportunities for creative expression
3. Avoiding ridicule, shame, or inducing guilt."

Hanoch McCarty, 1989

"Accepting ourselves begins with an honest look at who we are. We don't need to like everything we find... More and more over time, we can accept, appreciate, and celebrate ourselves as we are. We are each unique... Accepting ourselves does not discount the need for change and growth. Just the opposite; it is the first step we take when we want to change. We can decide to do something different after we accept who we are, where we are, and that we are capable of change."

California Task Force to Promote Self-Esteem and Personal and Social Responsibility

Highlights

1. Accepting who we are is the first step toward creating who we want to be.
2. Everyone is his/her own unique person.
3. Focus on what you can do, not what you cannot.

Funny Bones

I used to be indecisive, but now I'm not so sure.

Omni.

From the Sideline

My typxwritxr works quitx wxll xxcxpt for onx kxy. Somxtimxs it sxxms to mx that our group is likx my typxwritxr. Not all thx kxys arx working propxrly. You may say, "Wxll, I'm only onx pxrson. It won't makx much diffxrxncx." But you sxx, for thx group to bx xffxctivx it nxxds activx participation of xvxry pxrson. So thx nxxt timx you think your xffort isn't nxxdxd, rxmxmbxr my typxwritxr and say to yoursxlf, "I'm a kxy pxrson and nxxdxd vxry much!"

Unknown

Weighing the Facts

What Greenleaf Learning Says...

How we see ourselves is important to the creation of dreams. How possible we believe our dreams to be may result from the ultimate value we place upon ourselves. Even though I may be "able," I may not always value my abilities. While strengths can serve to heighten my image, they are not an assurance that I will recognize or admit my worth.

The power of creation is invaluable. Understanding that I have great influence over outcomes in my tomorrows empowers me to put forth efforts to "Make my dream come true." As I begin to exercise that freedom of choice, I realize that shaping "Who I am" is ultimately up to me. I can choose to "be shaped" primarily by external forces, or to carve the image myself.

Accepting the relatively few shortcomings each of us has opens opportunity to use the capabilities we do have. It's not so much *whether* we can do something, as it is *how* we're going to go about it. Significant people in our lives have a great deal to do with developing worth. Each of us impacts others, sometimes in ways we do not intend or recognize. Take care to assist others in the creation of their own worth. Don't take responsibility and do it for them... for that would be a short lived, dependent relationship. Help another to realize and exercise the authority they have over their future. You'll set them free.

Activity 4 : Breaking Patterns
Changing the Status Quo

"If something in your life has not worked for some time...

then by now you ought to be used to it."

Planting the Seeds

Foundation Mindset #2
Today Connects With
Tomorrow

The exercise on the next is designed to help you take a detailed look at the patterns you employ in your daily life. This is not to say that routines are necessarily healthy or not healthy, but only to demonstrate how they are formed. If we understand the components which serve to make up a standardized practice, we might better know how to alter it… should we choose.

Think of habits or procedures you follow in your daily life. Is it your rise and shine routine? Breakfast ritual? Getting dressed? Who you see, when? The route you take to work or to school? Shaving? Whatever your selection, jot it down in the first box.

Now, consider the components that may be a part of your routine. Several are listed within the boxes and prompts provided. For one type of habit or routine, time may be the most important aspect. For another, place. Still, a third may be the procedure or method, or steps you follow. By considering the components of what brings about a habit or routine, we can better understand why we do it as we do… and how to change, if desired.

This applies to individual habits as well as group behaviors. Consider changing something about the environment as you conduct a certain routine (the background music, the location, the lighting, smells which may be present and such). Would each/any alter the activity? For whom? In what ways?

This exercise could also be used to make decisions about how a group would like to form. It could serve to determine the underlying values or attributes which you would like to have persist. Ultimately, we identify with the patterns we follow.

Sculpting the Image ~ Changing the Status Quo

Describe something you do in the same way, at the same time, or in the same place.

Are there any SENSORY INPUTS you could change?

touch	taste	smell	sound	sight

How could you change the WAY you do it?

How could you change the TIME?

How could you change the PLACE?

How could you change the ENVIRONMENT or the CONTEXT?

We sometimes attach a movement or action to familiar circumstances ~ especially if they are emotion-laden. These are called "**sensory anchors.**"

Are there anchors present when this activity happens? Do you have a habit of crossing your legs, pulling at your ear, putting your hands over your mouth, or looking up at the sky?

This exercise may shed light on which aspects of a certain practice are heavily weighted... and which are not.

Which components could you change and not really affect the outcome?

Which ones if changed, would dramatically alter the outcome, or even prevent it from occurring?

What The Experts Say

8 Propositions for Success

1. All large scale change is ultimately "LOCAL IMPLEMENTATION."
2. Change is LEARNING ~ loaded with uncertainty.
3. Change is a JOURNEY, not a blueprint.
4. Change is RESOURCE HUNGRY.
5. PROBLEMS ARE OUR FRIENDS.
6. SEEKING ASSISTANCE is a sign of intelligence.
7. Change requires POWER TO MANAGE.
8. Change is SYSTEMIC.

Fullan and Miles, 1991

Highlights

1. By considering the components of what brings about a habit or a routine, we can better understand why we do it as we do... and how to change, if desired.
2. Some daily rituals make our lives manageable. Others have outlived their usefulness.

Funny Bones

I was up all night

wondering where the sun went when it set.

Finally... it dawned on me.

From the Sideline

HABIT	=	Hard to get rid of
ABIT	=	Still have "A-BIT"
BIT	=	Still have a "BIT"
IT	=	Still have "IT"

Weighing the Facts

What Greenleaf Learning Says...

Routines. Policies. Consistency. Status Quo. Rituals. Procedures. Rules. Standards. Regular. Ordinary. Established. Typical. System. Order. Same Time ~ Same Situation. Set.

There are so many ways to regulate our lives, and bring some semblance of security to our chosen path. Patterns are there for good reasons. They make our lives predictable and more comfortable ~ even the negative or unproductive patterns. Whether or not we decide to alter a pattern is not the issue. Why we continue with the habits we embrace is important to understand and be aware of. How to form new, desired routines and procedures is invaluable.

Some daily rituals make our lives manageable. Others have outlived their usefulness. Taking time to examine the patterns we have formed in our lives does not mean we must "upgrade" or make them better. It does afford us the awareness to be deliberate about that which we do... and that which we decide against doing. When change does become needed, then the basis for beginning the process may be more apparent.

Change is traditional. Things always change, that's why we establish routines. They help us cope with the ever changing world. We create stability in our surroundings as a natural behavior. Since change is not likely to go away, altering the status quo in small, incremental ways may be a "healthy habit" to consider ~ on a standard, routine basis.

Activity 5 : I Don't Matter

WHEN WE BELIEVE WE DON'T MAKE A DIFFERENCE...

The Outcome May Be Tragic.

Planting the Seeds

Foundation Mindset #3
I Make A Difference

When we fail to see the connection between what we do today... and outcomes in our tomorrows, we tend to invest little. We are motivated to put forth effort only when we believe one of two things:

1. Given reasonable effort, I can achieve, and
2. The achievement is of value to me.

The exercise on the following page is designed to show children how we cause differences in our lives. We all make a difference... in the life of at least one other person. Recognizing that gives me value ~ a sense of worth. Writing down a goal, and then taking a few moments to determine a couple of things I might deliberately do to help make it happen, shows how I am important in creating outcomes. The examples of negative actions serve to demonstrate two things. First, I have a choice of actions ~ to either support or hamper my success. Second, there are clearly some things I might do to promote my own failure ~ or sense of being unworthy.

Knowing both what is constructive and destructive to my goal empowers me to make a decision. Whether the goal be for today or for the month, the process causes me to look at how to get from where I am... to a desired place I wish to be. I do make a difference!

Sculpting the Image ~ I Can Make A Difference

Connecting My Today With My Tomorrow

NAME

GOAL ~ Describe something you would like to do or you would like to become.

POSITIVE " + "	NEGATIVE " - "
Describe 3 things you can do that WOULD help reach your goal.	Describe 3 things that would NOT help reach your goal.
1.	1.
2.	2.
3.	3.

What The Experts Say

"[Every child has] the need to feel potent, able to achieve something, able to succeed... to define a desired future and be able to attain it. [Self control and power] suffer when the teacher makes all the important decisions or manipulates the class into rubber stamping...; when grades are averaged; when the student has no input into the choice of topics or study methods."

To reduce a feeling of powerlessness:

1. "Reduce blame, guilt and fault-finding. Don't focus on the ERROR, focus on the SOLUTION.
2. Increase responsibility. THE ABILITY TO RESPOND, to cope with the situation.
3. Don't focus on the past. Focus on the PRESENT and the IMMEDIATE FUTURE because it EMPOWERS."

Hanoch McCarty, 1989

"Every child or youth should be deliberately engaged in designing and directing some change in their own life. This elevates the dignity and importance of learning as well as honoring informational and self-directed learning."

Dr. Gary Phillips, 1989

Highlights

1. We all make a difference.
2. We need to take time to recognize the ways in which we matter to ourselves and to others.
3. Children need to hear not only that they matter, but specifically how they make a difference ~ so they can repeat the positive actions.

Funny Bones

**"I am an underachiever...
but I've never been very good at it !"**

From the Sideline

Victor Frankl *

"What all of us want is to be set free. The man who sinks his pickaxe into the ground wants that stroke to mean something. The convict's stroke is not the same as the prospector's stroke… for obvious reasons. The prospector's stroke has meaning and the convict's has none. It would be a mistake to believe that prison exists at that place where the convict's stroke is dealt. Prison is not a mere physical horror. It is not just being locked up. Prison, is using your pickaxe to no purpose. That makes a prison. We all yearn to escape that prison."

* Taken from the book, "Man's Search for Meaning."

Weighing the Facts

What Greenleaf Learning Says...

When a child or adult portrays an "I don't matter" attitude, they are exhibiting a feeling of unimportance. The disposition of insignificance reduces one to a primary role of spectator or disruptor, rather than participant or contributor. It prompts us to indicate that things "*outside*" of us are controlling our experiences and outcomes, as opposed to "*internal*" factors or personal effort.

Simply telling someone they matter may feel a bit better, but requires evidence if sustained impact is desired. The exercise in this section depicts the need to clearly see the relationship between our investment of the moment (motivation to act) and potential outcomes later on. The amount of time until results are reasonably expected and the magnitude of the goal is within our reach, are usually determined by prior experiences. We need to build multiple, smaller achievements before undertaking larger ones.

Help your child (spouse, friend, or self) target something (reasonable or attainable) they would like to see happen. Then, take a few minutes to choose several ways s/he could attempt generating the outcome they desire ~ as well as ways they can deter the probability of success. This conscious activity will help establish a feeling of empowerment ~ and, ultimately, a series of accomplishments that creates a history of "can-do" experiences.

Activity 6 : Inviting Mistakes
Fear of Failure

YOU FELL DOWN WHEN YOU FIRST TRIED TO WALK.

Babe Ruth struck out 1330 times in hitting 714 home runs.

A failure a day, keeps complacency away.

Ready, Fire, Aim, Re-fire, Aim.... Re-fire...
Anything worth doing is worth doing poorly at first. Dr. Gary Phillips

The only time you can't afford to fail,
is the last time you try. Charles Kettering

Planting the Seeds

Foundation Mindset #3
I Make A Difference

There is failure in everything we do. Even when we enjoy success, there have been failures along the way. The exercise on the following page is designed to experience failure through success, overcoming the tendency to place too much credence in a debilitating fear factor.

First, we begin with something we have already accomplished. We have achieved success, so let's look at *how* we got there. Step two is to reflect back upon the process we went through. Somewhere along the way we found resistance. We ran into setbacks, and either renewed our commitment to purpose or changed our path to a valued one, which looked more promising. Perhaps, we made mistakes and had to start over again. One way or another, we persisted.

The third step is to examine the feelings we had when we experienced this pitfall in our plans (setbacks or mistakes are temporary delays to success. They become failures only if we accept them as undesired and unchangeable). The final step is to recall what we did to get beyond the mistake or setback, to bring about the accomplishment cited initially in the exercise.

Dealing with failure in our past and examining the accompanying feelings allows us to understand the process of overcoming obstacles. Once in perspective, we realize that "***Failure is what we do on the way to success.***"

Sculpting the Image ~ **Fear of Failure**

Failure is what we do on the way to success.

Describe something of importance you have ACCOMPLISHED.

What were some of the setbacks & mistakes along the way?

How did that make you feel?

What did you do as a result?

What The Experts Say

"Perceiving failure as caused by lack of effort allows students the possibility of future success with additional effort... We put forth effort if we believe that the effort will influence the outcome... Consequently, [if children are to be successful] they must believe that when they expend effort ~ something they completely control ~ they will experience success... 'If I think I can, I might; if I think I can't, I'm right."

M. Hunter & G. Barker "If at First..."

"People do not invest effort on tasks that do not lead to valued outcomes even if they know they can perform the tasks successfully, and they do not invest effort on even highly valued tasks if they are convinced that they cannot succeed no matter how hard they try... Effort and persistence are greater in individuals who set goals of moderate difficulty level, who seriously commit themselves to pursuing these goals, and who concentrate not on avoiding failure but on achieving success."

Jere Brophy, Synthesis of Research on Motivation

Highlights

1. Failure is what you do on the way to success.
2. It is not failure we fear, but the idea of being a failure.
3. A single mistake or setback is not what we fear, but rather, the notion of repeatedly failing. We need to break the habit of failure as a probable outcome.

Funny Bones

The Definition of Failure:
A kamikaze pilot on his third mission.

From the Sideline

"There is a time in every man's education when he arrives at the conviction that envy is ignorance; that imitation is suicide; that he must take himself for better for worse as his portion; that, though the wide universe is full of good, no kernel of nourishing corn can come to him but through his toil bestowed on that plot of ground which is given to him to till. The power which resides in him is new in nature, and none but he knows what that is which he can do, nor does he know until he has tried."

Ralph Waldo Emerson

Weighing the Facts

What Greenleaf Learning Says...

Failure followed by failure, followed by failure. Most have been there. We recognize the time(s) in our lives when failures seemed to be the main course, and success wasn't on the menu. Though we wanted to change our diet, the effort needed to alter course so often appeared overwhelming, or impossible. Slowly... we begin to believe there is little we can do about it ~ we begin to feel insignificant in the scheme of things, and diminish our perception of self worth.

When we think about movement (things changing from one place to another, from one idea or behavior to another), we might agree that things most often stay where they are. In other words, it is easier to keep things as is, than put forth energy to change them. However, the corollary is also true. If things move, they like to keep moving. Once we get off the ground, flying is easy. It's getting airborne that appears so difficult ~ especially when we're downtrodden.

Bottom Line **Things like to keep doing what they're already doing.** It takes equal energy to *stop* something in motion as it does to *start* motion.

If you're going to accept "*the way things are*," why not get them on a track for success first. Then, go ahead and live with repeated successes. It's just as easy as living with repeated failures. The only difference is where you choose to begin. "Success breeds success," really happens!

Activity 7 : Make Me Feel Worthwhile

WON'T SOMEBODY INVEST?

Sometimes I feel unnoticed. I come. I go. Unless I make trouble, no one seems to pay attention. How do I try out ideas and get to know who I am... who I want to be, if nobody takes notice?

"How can I stand up, if I don't know what I stand for?"

Planting the Seeds

Foundation Mindset #4
Someone Believes In Me

Having worth. Feeling as though there is something we do well. Knowing our ideas and concerns are important. Having a sense of accomplishment. These are all components... integral parts of being valued. Even though we may believe these things to be true, it is affirming to have others illuminate them. Taking notice, and committing the achievement(s) to some form of expression that can be shown to others, is like a confirmation that it must be so.

The exercise on the following page, "Hall of Fame," is designed to highlight an activity or accomplishment. The youth (or adult) "fills in the blanks." Find a snapshot of the person ~ or an illustration of the activity they have prospered at ~ or have them draw their own version of what it looks like... and enter it in the large, centered box.

Display the finished product in a place of prominence. Better yet, dedicate a location in your home, class or school where several could be placed. The setting for the completed exercise is as important as the sheet itself. Make the display inviting and worthy of such esteemed works. Framing could be a possibility.

Be sure the picture or illustration is positive, smiling, and indicative of the celebrated activity. And do just that... celebrate! Establish a ritual of admittance to the "coveted" Hall of Fame that denotes importance. Encourage participants to create a new one each month. As more and more collect, it will be easier to see that there are many things one can do well... "Hey, I must be worthwhile!"

Sculpting the Image ~ HALL OF FAME

Place a picture of his/her smiling face here.

What is the area of INTEREST or ENTERPRISE?

What The Experts Say

"The authorship of the thought process carries valued importance. Generating ideas and examples not only improves memory, it celebrates my ability to create and resolve. Finding and explaining examples strengthens knowledge and self-worth more than if another (especially an adult) generates the direction or solution."

Partially by Gorrell, et. al., 1989

"Self-concept depends on so many factors... It depends, in part, on the extent to which universal adolescent needs of affection, esteem, security, recognition, and belonging are met... It depends, in part, on us and how we make our [children] feel about themselves and their abilities. It depends, in part, on the assumptions we make about them that form our modus operandi... [Some children] are afraid to express their opinions because they don't respect their own feelings and instincts, or because they are afraid of opening themselves up to ridicule and embarrassment... [Self-worth] is so fundamental to human health that its implications permeate all we do with young people, peers, families, and society at large. It is so fundamental because self-definition predetermines how we perceive, react to, and act within the world around us."

Sometime A Shinning Moment

Highlights

1. I Am Worth It.
2. Pay attention to the things you do well.
3. By recognizing worth, you gain it.
4. Support is helpful when it validates your worth.

Funny Bones

"Ever have the feeling that in life, when you're finally holding all the cards, everyone else is playing chess?"

Gil Stern in the Wall Street Journal

From the Sideline

Not to understand the lad
He's not eager to be bad;
If the right he knew,
He would be as old as you.

Were he now exceeding wise,
He'd be just about your size;
When he does things that annoy,
Don't forget ~ he's just a boy.

Could she know and understand,
She would need no guiding hand;
But she's young and hasn't learned
How life's corner must be turned.

Doesn't know from day to day
There is more to life than play
More to face than a selfish whirl,
Don't forget, she's just a girl.

Being just a boy ways,
Have his disobedient days.
Willful, wild and headstrong, too;
He'll need guidance kind and true;
Things of value he'll destroy.

But reflect ~ he's just a boy.

Just a girl who needs a friend,
Patiently, kindly to the end;
Needs a parent who will show,
Hear the things she wants to know.

Take her with you when you walk,
Listen when she wants to talk,
Her companionship will unfurl,
Don't forget she's just a girl.

Anonymous

Weighing the Facts

What Greenleaf Learning Says...

"Make me feel important" was a principle first framed by Michael LeBouef in his book, *The Greatest Management Principal of All.* Feeling needed is an essential part of our being. In order to belong, we must believe we have something worthwhile to contribute, something in common with the desired group, organization or individual.

Certainly we all contribute, but knowing the value of our efforts is not always derived internally ~ at least at first. We al need support to validate our worth, our impact upon both the directions we choose for our own life and upon the lives of others.

So many go about their daily activities wondering if they do much of anything that matters. Too many do not see the fruits of their labors. When questioning our worth, doubting our importance or feeling discouraged, we tend to overlook our contributions and our value. Take the time today to compliment three people (one of whom you care little) with regard to something they do well. We all need to hear it. Then, take the time with a loved one. Help them to identify an area of worth to which they have been blinded or are unsure. Bring it to the forefront. Both of you will benefit. By recognizing worth, you gain it.

Activity 8 : Appreciation

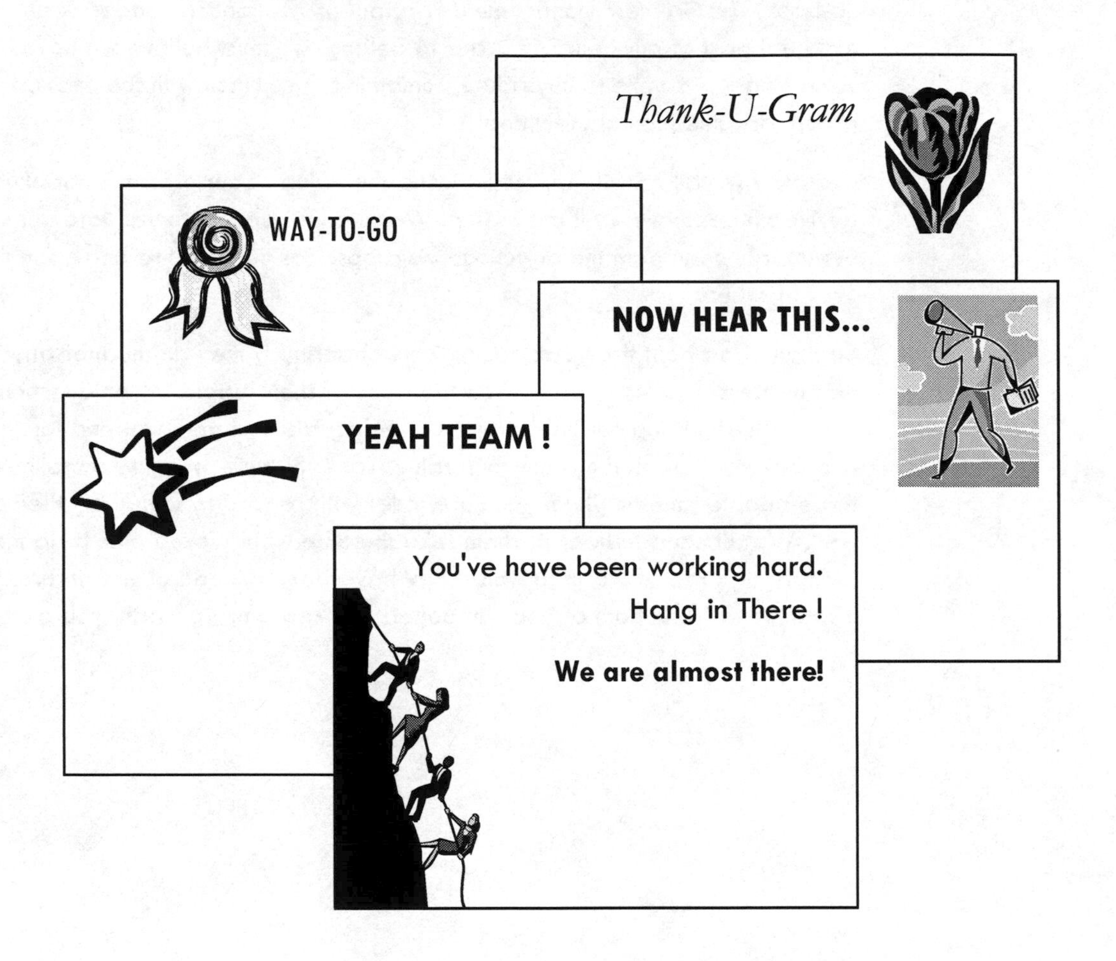

NOTES ~ NOT LETTERS

Planting the Seeds

Foundation Mindset #4
Someone Believes In Me

Few things mean more to us than being appreciated. When someone expresses a sincere acknowledgement or gratitude, we instantly respond with kind, warm, inner feelings. Connecting a positive emotion with an action or a relationship is a powerful way to recognize someone *and* to build a stronger, healthier relationship.

The examples and exercise on the following pages show some ways to help bring this about. If we connect a desired activity (the act of showing appreciation) with something that is *already taking place* regularly, then we are more apt to follow through. It is not that we do not feel appreciation or even that we do not want to express it. We get involved with our day and all its happenings… and tend to "get around to it" much later or not at all. Praise needs to be specific, sincere and *soon* to be most beneficial.

Attaching the desired action to a stable, routine event helps to prompt our memory. Once self-reminded, it is easier to act. It becomes a ritual; if this, then that. If we hold a meeting, we begin with writing appreciation cards to people. Each meeting could have a theme: Write to a parent, student, another educator, or community person; write to a troubled student, an often overlooked student or an artistic student; write to a community person who helps the school; write to a public figure, school board member or politician. The possibilities are endless ~ and the rewards are many.

If you wait too long, the impact of recognition rapidly diminishes.

Sculpting the Image ~ Rituals of Appreciation

PROMPT	ACTION
Morning Recess	Ask one child to linger before s/he goes out to play, and tell him/her something you have noticed which s/he has done well that morning.
Staff Meetings	Begin each meeting by writing notes to two people about something they have done well since the last meeting.
Arriving Home from School	Address your child with a greeting, and then a question about what s/he did that day that made him/her feel good.

PROMPT	ACTION
What are two rituals that occur in your home or school?	What could you do each time this ritual occurs that acknowledges, recognizes, or appreciates a parent, teacher, student, or administrator?
1.	1.
2.	2.

What The Experts Say

Many people feel a need to achieve. Volumes of management and motivation research and theory have been written on the encouragement, coaching, and productivity of people with a variety of tasks. David C. McClelland, Psychology Professor at Harvard University, talks of youth who seem compelled to achieve stating that, "The evidence suggests it is not because they are born that way, but because of special training they get in the home from parents who set moderately high achievement goals but who are warm, encouraging, and non-authoritarian in helping their children reach these goals."

David C. McClelland

"One of the most important goals we strive for as educators, parents, and mental health professionals is to help children develop respect for themselves and others. It is an ongoing process characterized by patience and one in which... all caring adults can play a vital role. Reinforcement is one of the keys. Recognition, praise, and kind words [of appreciation] help children and adults develop positive attitudes about themselves. As educators, we should emphasize a student's positive qualities. [Adults] who express positive attitudes apparently feel good about themselves and what they are doing. They automatically become positive role models for their students."

Karen Hayes Butler, Omaha, NE.

Highlights

1. We all need to feel appreciated.
2. The more often we feel appreciated, the more we find worth and meaning in our work and life.
3. Achievement can be nurtured by warm, encouraging, and goal setting adults.

Funny Bones

Would the thoughtful, nice person who did such a great job watering my lawn please come let me acknowledge you?
By the way, I'd also like to talk with you about the water in my living room, hallway, garage, car...!
Oh-oh...
I think she means me!

From the Sideline

"Children Need to Feel Appreciated and to Have Goals"

So the traditional nuclear family has changed. The national divorce rate has risen over the past 30 years. In a city of 20,000 people, 58% of the incoming kindergarten enrollees came from families in which the child lived with both parents. The percentage of wives working outside the home has gone from 32% to almost 75% and today, fewer children are doing less household chores than in the days of farm and factory. Today's family structure is altered for most and it exists in a very different milieu than days of old. With far less discretionary time available to families, parents now must be deliberate in structuring the kinds of activities and discussions needed to instill the desired values and ethics.

Without meaningful connection, little lasting learning takes place. Before a parent can offer a child guidance (before a teacher can offer education) a meaningful rapport must be established. Learning is directly connected to emotion and meaning. Our work as parents is to provide the meaningful connections between our children's experiences of today and the possibilities of tomorrow.

When a child is "at risk," s/he is usually feeling unimportant, unappreciated, misunderstood, and alone. When one member of a team feels left out, lacking influence, the team is "at risk" for lower performance. Similarly, when a member of the family is missing the sense of belonging, is feeling helpless or non-contributing, then all become "at risk" as a family unit.

It is relatively easy to notice the problems. The tough question is, "What are you willing to do today... to make tomorrow a little bit more the way you'd like it to be?"

Bob Greenleaf, Morning Sentinel. April 1990

Weighing the Facts

What Greenleaf Learning Says...

In our search for meaning and purpose, appreciation becomes a vital means of knowing. When another takes the time to notice our effort or accomplishment, we can begin believing that we do, in fact, make a difference.

It is a continual stream of people who willingly admit that feeling appreciated is one of the (if not the) most important motivators in their lives. Yet, the same people will tell you they receive very little. The exact amount of acknowledgement we get is not important.

The Bottom Line We all want more!

Most are quite earnest in their beliefs about and attempts to bestow appreciation on those in their lives of work or play. Quite simply, if something is important to us, if we value it, then we ought to find ways of honoring it enough to make it happen. Connecting the act of appreciating others to a daily or weekly ritual in our lives can create a ritual of appreciation. In little time, it will become automatic... which is just what we wanted in the first place.

Bibliography

Brain Based Education Networker. The Institute of Learning and Teaching, 449 Desnoyer, St. Paul, MN 55104-4915. Vol. 3, 1991.

Begly, Sharon et al. "Mapping the Brain." Newsweek. April 20, 1992. pp. 66-70.

Blakey, Elaine & Spencer Sheila. "Developing Metacognition." ERIC Digest, ED 327-218; Nov. 1990

Brophy, Jere. "Synthesis of Research on Strategies for Motivating Students to Learn." Educational Leadership. October 1987.

California Task Force to Promote Self-esteem and Personal and Social Responsibility. Toward A State of Esteem. Sacramento, CA January 1990.

Cauley, Kathleen M. & Frank B. Murray. "Structure of Children's Reasoning About Attributes of School Success & Failure." American Educational Research Journal. Fall 1982, Vol. 19, No. 3 p. 473-80.

Combs, Arthur. "Humanism, Education, and the Future." Educational Leadership, January 1978

Cramer, Jerome. "The Latest Research on Brian Growth Might Spark Learning in Your Schools." The American School Journal, August 1981.

Diagram Group, The. The Brain: A User's Manual. Perigee Books, G. P. Putnam, New York, 1982

Epstein, Herman T. "Learning to Learn: Matching Instruction to Cognitive Levels." Principal, May 1984.

Epstein, Joyce. "Hopkins Surveys of School and Family Connections: Questionnaires for Teachers, Parents and Students." Center for Research on Elementary and Middle Schools. Baltimore, MD: Johns Hopkins University.

Epstein, Joyce. "Parent Involvement: What Research Says to Administrators." Education and Urban Society, February 1987. p. 119-36. EF 351-802

Finkel, Larry. "Working with High Risk Students K-12: Leadership Styles Teaching Modalities and Supportive Supervision." ASCD tape, 1989.

Frieze, Irene H. "Casual Attributions and Information Seeking to Explain Success and Failure." Journal of Research in Personality. 10, 293-305, (1976).

Gardner, Howard. "Smartness vs Intelligence." Maine ASCD – Project Zero – Harvard.

Gelman, David et al. "Is the Mind an Illusion?" Newsweek. April 20, 1992 p. 71-72

Greenleaf, Robert K. "What's Left When You're Right?" Mainly Local. January/February 1985. Greenleaf Learning, P.O. Box 186, Newfield, ME 04056 www.greenleaflearning.com

Greenleaf, Robert K. & Rachel P. Rastrom. Working With Young People. Greenleaf Learning, P.O. Box 186, Newfield, ME 04056 www.greenleaflearning.com (1991)

Greenleaf, Robert K. "The Nation's Largest Casino" Mainly Local. September/October 1984. Greenleaf Learning, P.O. Box 186, Newfield, ME 04056 www.greenleaflearning.com

Greenleaf, Robert K. Series of five articles written for the Morning Sentinel on parenting and youth development. April 1990 Greenleaf Learning, P.O. Box 186, Newfield, ME 04056 www.greenleaflearning.com

Greenleaf, Robert K. "Self Esteem: Listen to the Artist Within." Presentation made to audiences on building and diminishing esteem. Greenleaf Learning, P.O. Box 186, Newfield, ME 04056 www.greenleaflearning.com (1995)

Greenleaf, Robert K. "Successful Kids – How do I get one?" Presentation made to audiences on today's youth. Greenleaf Learning, P.O. Box 186, Newfield, ME 04056 www.greenleaflearning.com (1995)

Greenleaf, Robert K. "The Anatomy of a Bomb: Youth Transitions to Adulthood." Presentation made to audiences on families, youth and the family system. Greenleaf Learning, P.O. Box 186, Newfield, ME 04056 www.greenleaflearning.com (1994)

Greenleaf, Robert K. "Brain Based Teaching: Building Excitement for Learning." Published 1995. Updated 2000, 2005. Greenleaf Learning, P.O. Box 186, Newfield, ME 04056 www.greenleaflearning.com

Greenleaf, Robert K. "Learning Groups and the POWER of 2." Published 1998. Greenleaf Learning, P.O. Box 186, Newfield, ME 04056 www.greenleaflearning.com

Gregorc, Anothony R. "Teaching/Learning Styles: Potent Forces Behind Them." Educational Leadership, January 1979.

Gregorc, Anothony R. "Style as a Symptom: A Phenomenological Perspective." Theory Into Practice, Vol. 23, No. 1.

Gregorc, Anothony R. "Learning Style/Brain Research: Harbinger of an Emerging Psychology." Student Learning Styles and Brain Behavior, Reston, VA: NASSP (Monograph), 1983.

Haglund, Elaine. "A Closer Look at the Brain As Related to Teachers and Learners." Peabody Journal of Education, July 1981, p. 225-234.

Hart, Lesile A. Human Brain, Human Learning. Longman Press, 1983. P.O. Box 20525, Village of Oak Creek, AZ 86341

Hart, Lesilie A. "Moving From 'Logic' to Brain Compatibility." The Brain-Based Networker, Summer 1990, Vol. 2, p. 2.

Hart, Lesilie A. "The Three Brains in the Classroom." The Brain-Based Networker, Summer 1990, Vol. 2, p. 2.

Henderson, Anne T. et al. "Beyond the Bakesale: An Educator's Guide to Working with Parents." Columbia, MD: The National Committee for Citizens in Education, 1986

Herrmann, Ned. "The Creative Brain Part II: A Revisit With Ned Herrmann." Training and Development Journal, December 1982, Vol. 36, No. 12, p. 74-88.

Hunter, Madelyn & George Barker. "If at First…'" Attribution Theory in the Classroom." Educational Leadership. October, 1987, p. 50-3. Image. April – June, 1981. Vol. XI, No. 2.

Jennings, Wayne B. "Infant Learning: Key to Understanding all Learning." The Brain-Based Networker. Summer, 1990. 2, 2.

Jennings, Wayne B. Brain-Based Education Networker. The Institute for Learning and teaching, 449 Desnoyer, St. Paul, MN 55104-4915. Vol. 3, 1994

Joyce, Bruce R. "Learning How to Learn." Theory into Practice. Vol 19, No. 1, Winter 1980, p. 15-27.

Languis, M. Saunders, T. and Tipps, S. "Brain & Learning: Directions in Early Childhood Education." Washington D.C. National Association for the Education of Young Children, 1980. p. 48.

Lebouef, Michael. "Imagineering." M.S. Library 153.43 L447J 1987.

Levy, Jerry. "Research Synthesis on Right and Left Hemispheres: We Think with Both Sides of the Brain." Educational Leadership, January 1983, p. 471-483

Lewis, Jerry M. "The Adolescent and the Healthy Family." Paper from Research and Training at Timberlawn Psychiatric Research Foundation. Dallas, TX.

Maranto, Gina. "The Mind Within the Brain." Discover, May 1984. pp.34-43.

McCarthy, Bernice. "The 4-Mat System, Teaching to Learning Styles with R/L Mode Techniques." Excel, Inc., Oak Brook, IL 1980

McCarty, Hanoch. "Self-Esteem: The Bottom Line With Students-At-Risk." Hanoch McCarty & Associates, Inc. 19800 Fairmount Boulevard, Cleveland, Ohio.

MacLean, Paul. "Brain Education: The Origins of Social & Cognitive Behaviors." A Child's Brain. Haworth Press Inc., p. 9-21, 1984.

Nicholls, John G. "Effort is Virtuous, but It's Better to Have Ability: Evaluative Responses of Effort and Ability." Journal of Research in Personality, 10, p. 306-15 (1976)

National School Boards Association. First Teachers: Parental Involvement in the Public Schools. Alexandria, VA. 1988.

Orvin, George. "Intensive Treatment of the Adolescent and His Family." New Hope, Charleston, SC.

Phillips, Gary. "27 Ways to Improve Classroom Instruction." National School Improvement, PO Box 1234, Issaquah, WA 98027.

Phillips, Gary. "Classroom Rituals for At-Risk Learners." National School Improvement Project, P.O. Box 11365, Bainbridge Island, WA. 98110.

Phillips, Gary. "What's A Parent To Do?" National School Improvement Project, P.O. Box 11365, Bainbridge Island, WA. 98110.

Quick, Harry D. "Brain Hemispheric Preferences of Five to Twenty-One Year Olds." Balance, inc, Creative Mind Systems, Wiscasset, Maine. 1985.

Rico, Gabriele Lusser. Writing the Natural Way. J.P. Tarcher, Inc. 9110 Sunset Blvd., Los Angeles, CA.

Rozek, Michael. "Fear of Failure." Your Company. Fall 1990.

Samson, Grace & Walberg Weinstein. "Academic and Occupational Performance: A Qualitative Synthesis." American Educational Research Journal. Series 84, Vol. 21, No. 2. p. 311-21.

Sears, Nedra C. & Dale M. Johnson. "The Effects of Visual Imagery on Spelling Performance & Retention Among Elementary Students." Journal of Educational Research. Mar/Apr. 1986. Vol. 70, No. 4, p 230-3.

Sometimes A Shining Moment. "They Understand the Role of Self-esteem." P. 233-240.

Sperry, Roger W. "The Great Cerebral Comissure." Scientific American, Freeman & Co., San Francisco, January 1964, Vol. 210, No. 1, p. 42-52

Sylwester, Robert. "Research on Memory: Major Discoveries, Major Educational Challenges." Educational Leadership, April 1985.

Taggert, William and Daniel Robey. "Minds and Managers: On the Dual Nature of Human Information Processing an Management." Academy of Management Review, 1981, Vol. 6, No. 2, p. 187-195

Taggert, William; Robey, Daniel; and Taggart, Barbara. "Decision Styles Education: An Innovative Approach." Exchange: The Organizational Behavior Teaching Journal, 1982, Vol. 7, No. 2, p. 17-24

Telzrow, Cathy F. "The Impact of Brain Development on Curriculum." The Educational Forum. May 1981, p. 471-83.

Torrence, E.P. Reynolds, C.R. "Your Style of Learning and Thinking." Gifted Child Quarterly, 1977, Vol. 21, p. 563-73.

Vitale, Barbara Meister. Unicorns Are Real, "A Right Brained Approach to Learning." Jalmar Press, Rolling Hills Estates, California, 1982

Walberg, Herbert J. "Improving the Productivity of America's Schools." Educational Leadership. May 1984.

Weaver II, Richard L. & Howard W. Cotrell. "Imaging: Insight Engineering." Ed 260-466. Bowling Green State University, Bowling Green, Ohio.

About the Author

Dr. Robert K. Greenleaf

Dr. Robert K. Greenleaf has served as a professional development specialist at Brown University. With experience in all grade levels K-16, he has 20 of years of service in public education ranging from Superintendent of Schools to Assistant Superintendent of Schools, District Coordinator of Student Aspirations, Elementary School Principal, Teacher, and Special Education Assistant. He has also taught at the College level.

President of Greenleaf Learning, founded in 1987, Bob specializes in educational strategies for understanding behaviors, building esteem and achievement, and brain-based learning for long-term memory and recall. Bob is the author of seven instructional books, as well as many articles. He is the recipient of the "Outstanding Educator Award" from the Waterville Public Schools in Maine. Bob holds a Doctorate in Education from Vanderbilt University, a Masters in Educational Administration, and a Bachelor's degree in Psychology.

A past member of the National Speakers Association and Toastmasters International, he won several area and district speech events in the 1980's. His primary work is in the translation of research into practical applications for educators.

Contact Information: www.greenleaflearning.com

BOOKS FOR SALE *Greenleaf & Papanek* Publications

COLLEGE EDITION
Stock ID: **ETS-C** Price: **$27**

GRADES 5-12 EDITION
Stock ID: **ETS-S** Price: **$27**

ENGAGING TODAY'S STUDENTS, What All Educators Need to Know & Be Able to Do

In these two editions of "Engaging Today's Students," we have examined the research around the learner of today, effective teaching practices, and the brain sciences that link to long-term memory and recall. We have observed hundreds of classroom lessons and activities, developed by an array of practicing educators. A strong indicator for how we organized this book was our deep commitment to learners ~ students as learners AND teachers as learners ~ and how we all can learn in significant and sustainable ways.

With a central focus on what today's learners require, we have created two editions, one with a focus on College level learners and the other referencing the needs of the grades 5-12 population of students. Each addresses the four essential learning components that drive student engagement.

Memory, Recall, the Brain & Learning

Explore ways of incorporating brain-based instruction in the classroom. The power of combining verbal and visual representations into powerful bi-modal memory packets. Over 40 teacher and student generated activities, organizers, templates, and strategies. Improve student performance!

Stock ID: **MRBL** Price: **$25**

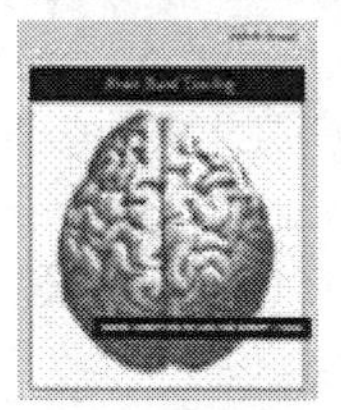

Brain Based Teaching

Explore teaching and learning through three overarching lenses: How can I "frame" (design) the learning circumstance or activity to INVITE ALL learners, to participate? How can I design the learning experience to CAUSE learner processing ~ the work required for sustained learning and recall? How do I engineer tasks that create opportunities for multiple PATHWAYS (connections) to be formed for integration, application, & recall?

Stock ID: **BBT** Price: **$24**

Coaching Reluctant Learners

This book provides today's middle and high school teachers with the tools they need to ensure classroom success for today's students in a practical framework ~ unit-by-unit, where both teacher and student can feel more successful. Embedded in this book are proven strategies, activities, examples, and a framework for units that will improve student motivation and performance.

Stock ID: **CRL** Price: **$27**

A Mastery Toolkit

Speaking directly to the student, this book explores the foundations of understanding, essential strategies, and learning tools to become motivated, independently engaged in the learning process, responsible for learning, and accountable for making good choices. The goal is to become a "Can Do" Student ~ a student who takes charge of their learning and empowers themselves in ways to be successful.

Stock ID: **AMT** Price: **$25**

Creating & Changing Mindsets

If rational behavior was the basis for human interaction and the mysteries of learning and development were well understood ~ this book wouldn't be needed. Clear strategies to assist "shifts" in attitude and behavior are included. The question, "will this change last?" plagues us every year. Here's how to impact changes within a month's time... for long-term, sustained differences!

Stock ID: **CCM** Price: **$24**

Greenleaf & Papanek **Publications**
PO Box 186 Newfield, Maine 04056

BOOK ORDER FORM

Please mail this form, to the above address, with a check, or

Fax a Purchase Order to:
fax 847.615.9958

bob@greenleaflearning.com
tel 207.793.8675

doris@tailoredlearningtools.com
tel 847.615.9957

NAME

CO/ORG/SCHOOL

ADDRESS

CITY

STATE/ZIP CODE

EMAIL

TELEPHONE

CHECK or PO #

DATE

Make checks payable to **GREENLEAF LEARNING**.

For more information, please visit our websites:
www.greenleaflearning.com
www.tailoredlearningtools.com

For Discounts on Bulk Orders Over 10 Books Total: Call 207.793.8675

INSTRUCTIONS

1. Enter the "Quantity" of each book you are buying
2. Add the total number of books and multiply by the "discount" amount using the "Discount Calculator"
3. Multiply "Quantity" x "Price" and enter the amounts due for each book in the "Totals" column
4. Add the extended total in the "Subtotal" box
5. Subtract the quantity discount and then add shipping fees to arrive to your final "TOTAL COST."

DISCOUNT CALCULATOR

2 books total	=	**$1** discount per book
3 books total	=	**$2** discount per book
4 books total	=	**$3** discount per book
5-10 books total	=	**$4** discount per book

STOCK ID	QUANTITY	PRICE	TOTALS
ETS-C college		x $27	=
ETS-S grades 5-12		x $27	=
MRBL		x $25	=
BBT		x $24	=
CRL		x $27	=
AMT		x $25	=
CCM		x $24	=
discount	x =	**subtotal**	=
		less discount	-
		total	=
		shipping 1-4 books	+ $3.50
		additional shipping for more than 4 books add .50 cents each	+
		Canada add $3.00	+
		TOTAL COST	=